MW00622511

Praise for *12 Rules for Manliness*

"The world needs more manliness, men who are rugged and courageous, yet loving and merciful. Bear Woznick is such a guy, and this book is a great way for men to kick-start the adventure of learning to be heroic again. I highly recommend this book and pray that it will help bring an end to the woke ideology that has emasculated so many men in our times."

—Fr. Donald Calloway, M.I.C.
Author, *Consecration to St. Joseph*

"I have long admired Bear's passion for virtue while building up the Body of Christ through his adventurous endeavors. Now, more than ever, we need men who are willing to step up to be the 'strong, virtuous cowboys' Bear describes in this book. A fantastic way to inspire masculinity: the Wild West, the path less taken, and lives of hardened, humble men. Well done, Bear!"

—Rose Rea
Founder of *Radiant* and *Valiant* magazines;
co-author of *Defend Us in Battle: The True Story of U.S. Navy SEAL Medal of Honor Recipient Michael A. Monsoor*

"What young boy hasn't widened his eyes watching a cowboy charging across the plains on a fleet-footed horse and thought, 'Someday I want to be a cowboy'? What is the allure? The cowboys of legend were rugged men who worked hard and fought for justice. With chivalry, they bowed to God, defended their children, and honored their women. Our culture is losing the image and respect of the masculine man with a fist of steel in a velvet glove. Men are belittled, priests are slandered, and fathers are mocked. For a society to be strong, young men need heroic models. As Bear

Woznick explains so well, we need to reclaim the cowboys among us—godly, masculine men who can inspire the next generation of manly young men (and the gals who admire them)."

—Steve Ray
CatholicConvert.Com

"Somehow the idea got out that masculinity is the same as machismo. It's not. It's half the story of sanctity. Bear Woznick is here at last to set the record straight."

—Michael Aquilina
Writer on the Early Church Fathers

"Bear gets right to the heart of the modern-day version of spiritual warfare over truth and the assault on the family, with a laser focus on the lies of the woke culture about men and their participation in salvation. Bear's signature easy-to-read style and well-chosen stories illuminate the path to salvation through Jesus Christ and His presence in the Eucharist, being with us and guiding us through the Holy Spirit 'until the end of the age.'"

—Scott French, M.D.
The Magis Center

"Both of my grandfathers were Texas cowboys. Tough, strong men. Builders. Dreamers. God-fearing. The kind of men who would give you the shirts off their own backs. I hear stories about these kinds of men that often end with 'They don't make them like that anymore.' This kind of heroic grit runs deep in the blood of us men. Bear helps us to recall these natural, God-given traits and virtues and to combine them with supernatural Christian grace. Rediscover this strength, man of God, and use it to serve!"

—Mark Hartfiel
Vice president of Paradisus Dei
(That Man Is You! men's program)

"In *12 Rules for Manliness*, Bear Woznick guides young men on the great adventure toward becoming kind, gentle, strong, daring, and Godly men. Saddle up; you are in for a wild ride."

—Jason Jones
Founder of the Vulnerable People Project

"From a man named Bear, one could expect strong advice for making strong men. And Bear delivers. From a life of God-guided true manhood, he shapes men into being who God meant them to be, every day for the long ride home."

—**Dr. Ray Guarendi**
Host of *The Doctor Is In*;
author of *Taught by Ten, Living Calm,*
and many other books

12 Rules for Manliness

Other books by Bear Woznick
from Sophia Institute Press:

A Surfer's Guide to the Soul

Deep Adventure

Bear Woznick

12 Rules FOR Manliness

Where Have All the Cowboys Gone?

SOPHIA INSTITUTE PRESS
Manchester, New Hampshire

Sophia Institute Press
Box 5284, Manchester, NH 03108
1-800-888-9344
www.SophiaInstitute.com

Sophia Institute Press® is a registered trademark of Sophia Institute.

hardcover ISBN 978-1-64413-636-2

ebook ISBN 978-1-64413-637-9

Library of Congress Control Number: 2023941811

First printing

Contents

Dedication

It was my cowgirl wife, Cindy, who inspired this book when she introduced me to the song "Where Have All the Cowboys Gone?"

As we drank our morning coffee on the beach or took our afternoon walk along the sand, I would bring up the topic I was writing about at that time. And she would share with me that down-to-earth womanly perspective that only a cowgirl can give.

As the chapters rolled out, she patiently read through them and gave me her notes. More than that, she gave me her belief in me and her encouragement. One thing about my bride: she knows how to make a man feel like a man. It makes me want to rise to her level of belief in me.

Mahalo, Tandem Girl, for all your encouragement, wisdom, and patience as we focused so much time and energy on this project. I pray that your wildest dreams will come true.

Bear

Foreword

Jesus knew a thing or two about herding. While He spoke little of being a cowboy, He said much about being a sheep herder. He knew what it was like to suffer for the sheep, to defend them from starvation, and to keep them from being the food of wolves. He knew about sacrificing and laying down His life. As a carpenter, He had calloused hands, perhaps making shepherds' staffs or building corrals. Though there is no record of His mounting a horse, he knew how to ride regally on the colt of an ass, a beast of burden. He carried our burdens on His own back when He carried the Cross, and He shed His blood in that place outside the city where grittiness was well known. He never had a wife, but He embraced the whole world in the most intimate nuptial embrace imaginable, so that all could be one in Him.

Very often, we have a tendency to tame Jesus and to domesticate Him. But He was and is wild in His pursuit of us sinners. He is zealous and will stop at nothing to bring us into His beloved flock.

As we thank Bear Woznick for his insightful challenge to rediscover the manhood and fatherly care that are so needed in today's world, we see that he points us always to Jesus, the

Good Shepherd, the King of kings, the Lord of lords, and the "Cowboy of all cowboys," who feeds us with Himself and His everlasting love.

Bishop Larry Silva
Bishop of Honolulu

12 Rules for Manliness

Where Have All the Cowboys Gone?

Everyone has it in their power to say, this I am today, that I will be tomorrow. The wish, however, must be implemented with deed.
— Louis L'Amour, *The Walking Drum*

As my wife, Cindy, and I drove along the ocean by Diamond Head, near our home in Waikiki, a song came on the country radio station. Cindy reached over to turn it up and said, "You are gonna love this song." The voice of Paula Cole captured the longing of so many women today for a real man as she sang "Where Have All the Cowboys Gone?"

> Where is my John Wayne?
> Where is my prairie song?
> Where is my happy ending?
> Where have all the cowboys gone?

That struck a deep chord on my heartstrings. When I was a young boy, all my heroes were cowboys. They sat tall in the saddle, stood strong, and shot straight. While I was busy playing sports, surfing, and doing odd jobs around our little two-store town of Corralitos (Little Corral) near Santa Cruz, California, my sisters Dawn and

Tammy would rush home from school each day to ride our dark-maned buckskin horse, aptly named Buck. When I was a junior in high school, we moved to Waco, in the heart of Texas, and this California beach boy got a dose of even more of that cowboy mystique. The *boy howdys* and the unending Texas colloquialisms and philosophizing couldn't help but spur me on to the cowboy ways.

My wife started riding her pony, Dusty, when she was just six years old and then graduated to her first real horse, Peanut. She wore only cowgirl boots until she became a cheerleader in her north Florida high school of only one hundred students. She could ride standing up, Roman style, and was a trick rider and a barrel racer. She is a real cowgirl. She can saddle a horse, hitch up a horse trailer, clean the barn, and "explain things" to a stubborn stallion.

In fact, much of this book consists of trails of thoughts that she and I have traveled over, pondered about, and sifted through. That's what gives this book that cowboy kick with the spurs to say, "You can do this. You can be the hero you know you are called to be; the hero you want to be; the hero the world needs." So let's saddle up. The world needs more real men. The world needs more cowboys.

When I was growing up, my family spent our summer vacations riding in our station wagon on two-lane highways over the Sierras, through the desert, and across the Rockies. Then it was on into the Great Plains, through Nevada, Utah, Idaho, Wyoming, Montana, and into the Dakotas and even Minnesota, which is where my parents' roots were. It was not unusual in those days to see cowboys driving their herds along those highways, even stopping traffic for long periods as they eased their "doggies" across the road.

When we stopped for gas or for a burger at an A&W Root Beer stand, we would see those cowboys leaning against a wall or standing with one foot up on a dried-out porch, rolling a cigarette. Sometimes they would notice me noticing them. I was thrilled when they nodded to me and maybe tipped a hat to my mom and my sisters. They were just like my heroes in the western movies and TV shows that we all watched. (Today, if you get off the Internet highway and the interstate highway, you can still find them.)

I aspired to be like Roy Rogers and the Lone Ranger. I practiced my dive-and-roll while pulling my gun from its holster and firing like Little Joe Cartwright on *Bonanza*—although, now that I think about it, Little Joe was shot eighteen times, so maybe just ducking would work better. I wanted to live up to John Wayne's words: "You are born a boy, but you got to become a man." I wanted to live up to their Cowboy Code. It seemed that the men, the fathers around me, all sought to do the same.

I wanted to be tough like those men, to be fair like them, and I wanted to stand for something. I would practice my quick draw, swiftly pulling my cap gun from my Rowdy Yates holster, hung low and tied down, as Clint Eastwood wore his in *Rawhide*. I practiced my roping skills on fence posts and lawn furniture. Times have changed, and movies have changed, but even George Lucas said that *Star Wars* was just a cowboy movie set in space.

Cowboys were lean and as leathery as their saddles. Their calloused hands showed they were real cowhands. They didn't talk much because those long hours of solitude in the saddle kind of settled in their souls. They wore their hats low to block out the blazing sun. They wore big bandanas, not just because they were "perty" but because they came in handy to keep dust out of their lungs on trail drives, to bind up wounds, and even to bring water to their horses to drink. Sometimes cowboys tied it wet around their necks to keep themselves cool.

I saw cowboy virtue portrayed on TV, but I also saw it lived out every day by the men around me who exuded reliability and strength all mixed in with honor and humility. I saw tough, hardworking, faithful men all around me—men like Jake and Joe down at the Corralitos Market, with Joe behind the meat counter, always with a meat cleaver in his hand and a smile on his face. Jake was always busy manning the shelves. The men of our little town called themselves the "Padres," and they were fathers to all of us. A lot of them belonged to the volunteer fire department, too, or served as Scout leaders.

We did not have organized sports, but there was a bag full of bats, balls, and bases that we could get from the back of the market and then go play in the dirt field next to the Grange hall. These men were famous for the big pancake breakfast that people came to from all over, and in time the pancake breakfast became the destination for the big annual Watsonville Fly-In event for hundreds of private pilots. This is where I first learned to crack an egg open without breaking the yolk, and I learned when and how to flip a pancake. I was in the company of good men—or at least men who strived to be good.

Life then seemed idyllic, but the reality was, those were tough times. But the men were tough too. They rose up to life's adversity. They found fulfillment not so much in their "careers" but in knowing that their hard work made their families' lives a bit easier, a bit better.

Remember the saying:

> Soft times make for soft men.
> Soft men make for tough times.
> Tough times make for tough men.
> Tough men make for soft times.

Where are we right now in this continuum? I reckon we are somewhere in those first two lines. But there are tough men still today. St. Augustine said it best, as usual: "Bad times, hard times, this is what people keep saying; but let us live well, and times shall be good. We are the times: Such as we are, such are the times."[1]

Men seemed to keep each other in line, and girls made their men wait till marriage before (as they would say) "losing their virginity." Virginity was something to be cherished until marriage. Women had a solidarity with each other to draw that line and hold that line. To "shack up," as it was called, was scandalous and very rare. In fact, most of us youngsters did not even know the "facts of life" until one of our parents taught us in the fifth or sixth grade—unless, of course, we were raised on a ranch.

The men in those days knew that their families counted on them to protect and provide for them. There was no nanny state taking care of them, as if they were helpless victims. No: they manned up and did what needed to be done.

For the most part, moms were there in the home to raise the children. Practically all of our moms were there when we kids came home after school to play. Men opened car doors for women, and the women slid in across the bench seat to cozy up to the men while choosing the radio station.

Children were not the royalty of the family or the center of the universe. They knew that the world did not revolve around them. They were both loved and disciplined. They had a respect for authority, and when they asked, "Why?" parents simply said, "Because I said so." They knew they had a role to play to keep the family running smoothly with chores of their own.

---

[1] St. Augustine, Sermon 311, 8.

The men I knew growing up were like rocks, immovable and yet, to some degree, huggable. The men knew their duty, and they did it. They manned up by giving themselves to those they loved. They had been toughened by the times. Some were born during the Great Depression. Some served in World War I or World War II or the Korean War. They pursued a path of honor and virtue.

When I was in college, I remember, someone once asked my friend Jerry Cohn if he was a Christian, and he looked back, perplexed, and said, "Well, yeah. I am an American." That is not to say that there was no respect for other religions, but Christianity was known to be our country's backbone. It gave us our moral values and our work ethic.

I am not suggesting that we go back to living that way of life. But I am saying, instead of going "Back to the Future," as the movie title goes, we need to go "Back to the Virtue." Those virtues have been held by great men in every age and in every place. They were written down by men like Plato and Aristotle. The four cardinal (or moral) virtues are justice, temperance, fortitude, and prudence. Twenty centuries ago, St. Paul added the virtues of faith, hope, and love.

I am not saying we should go back and wear Greek robes or cowboy spurs. But this book is meant to unroll those virtues like a cowboy's bedroll, especially as they're seen in the light of the cowboy's campfire and in his life and work. They're Rules for Manliness, inspired by the manliest of men. I would count real Christians as the manliest among them. Christians have always had to swim upstream against the culture of the day. These rules are something every man should teach his sons. Uncles should demonstrate them to their nephews.

To this end, our Bear School of Manliness at DeepAdventure.com has video, audio, and written content that dads can study for themselves along with other men in our Man Cave Community site and through our monthly Zoom meetups with other men, and they also can easily lead their sons on a journey of discovery through them too.

Where have all the cowboys gone? Where did we go off the rails? The pill, sexual permissiveness, pornography, the "swipe right, swipe left," instant-gratification culture, and the lack of *responsibility* lets boys saunter through life without ever becoming men. Once women stopped waiting for marriage during the sexual revolution in the sixties, all Hell broke loose and demons raged and rampaged through our society. Boys who are old enough to be men instead seek pleasure and escape to gaming, drinking, sex, drugs, and rock and roll.

Today's man-boys have boxes of participation trophies that they got from playing soccer instead of football—because "football is too violent." They move those boxes to a corner of the basement when they move down there because they "need their space"—instead of moving out into their own apartments! In school, they learn liberal ideologies and false historical narratives, instead of reading, writing, math, and history. They learn to despise the "foolish, bigoted superstitions" of Christianity and to embrace noble, high-minded atheism.

They grow up feeling that they are owed a comfortable life, coddled, cuddled, and nurtured by their parents, their schools, and the government, protected from consequences. They realize too late that the degree to which they are "taken care of" is the degree to which they lose their freedom. Eventually, they find that the "safe place" they are provided with is really just a prison. They take offense at whatever the new fad is to take offense at, instead of living by St. Paul's assertion that "love does not take offense" (see 1 Cor. 13:5). Their biggest risk is trying something new at Starbucks. Their epitaph will read: "Died at age eighteen, buried at age seventy."

At best, they are only nice guys. They are far from being good men. It is only when a boy faces adversity and accepts responsibility for himself and others that he grows to be a man. As John Wayne said in the movie *McLintock!*, "To be a gentleman, you first have to be a man."

Some say that these historical values, these traditions, are just meant for the ash heap. But every cowboy knows, upon returning to camp after his night watch on a trail drive, that within the ashes of the firepit there are hot embers—embers he can fan into flame. Men, we need to fan into flame the hidden embers in the ashes of traditional virtues to put a fire in our belly that will make us strong and maybe even a little dangerous. Be the kind of man who, when you roll out of bed in the morning, makes the demons cower and think, "Oh no, he's up."

It's time for us men to be the heroes that we know in our guts we are created to be. The Latin root for the word *virtue* is *vir*, which means "man." It is the very nature, the call, the purpose of a man to live out virtue. A man comes hardwired with a call to virtue, to even be virtue itself—to be manly. He is born, of course, with a fallen nature, but there is a yearning in him for virtue.

Women have their role in this too. See in your man that hero to be called out by you and drawn out by you. Every man, when he is up against it, needs a woman, a cheerleader, someone who believes in his virtue and strength as he rises to the challenge. After all, it was women, more than the six-shooter, who tamed the West. Cowboys respected women and desired their respect. They sought to live up to the virtue the women expected in them.

When I was growing up, the men did not try to be nice. They wanted to be good men with a good name. Men today need to pursue virtue. We need to pursue doing the right thing for the right reason and at the right time. We need to be patient when necessary but always leaning in and being proactive. This was the standard that was set in my youth. Just like the cowboys, who live by a code, those men lived by this unspoken way.

They took their families to church on Sunday mornings and to a neighbor's house or to the park or the beach for a barbecue on Sunday afternoons. They played cards, drank, and smoked cigarettes, which they dropped into their beer cans. (I found that out the hard way.) They played music and sang and had fun. Families gathered together.

I know it all sounds unreal. And to be fair, many people's lives were not like this. But mine was, and yours can be too. The common bond of pursuing virtue makes for strong people, strong families, and strong friends. In Hawaii, where I live, that sense of *ohana* (family) and extended family is central to our culture. When I was growing up, families were self-reliant, but when the need arose, they also relied on each other. And so I wonder, where did all these good men go?

Where have all the cowboys gone? We need men to cowboy up now more than ever.

All My Heroes Were Cowboys

They were men who put others first, who rode for the
brand, who persevered, who fought while wounded.
They were dangerous. Not to be trifled with. They were
men who persevered on their "Long Ride Home."

– Louis L'Amour

Cowboys were men who put others first, who rode for the brand.
They got the job done, come hell or high water. They persevered
and kept fighting, even when wounded. They were as dangerous
as a rattlesnake or a cornered mountain lion. They were not to
be taken lightly.

Deep in his heart, every man senses that call to live the heroic
way, to champion a cause greater than himself. So he reaches out
to God, who he knows is greater than he. Even in everyday life,
he goes beyond the ordinary, and he rides high in the saddle of
his principles and dreams. He cowboys up.

Cowboys, more than anything, are the real thing. What you
see is what you get—humble yes, but with no apologies for who
they are. And they *know* who they are because they know what
they believe and what they stand for. Most have a faith in God

that comes only from the solitude of sleeping under the stars as they waterfall in a slow-moving cascade that you can almost reach out and touch.

As can be seen on my motorcycle-based EWTN TV series, *Long Ride Home with Bear Woznick*, bikers have a lot in common with cowboys. They have a true brotherhood, and yet they also have a lot of time for solitude in the saddle. As with cowboys, their faith deepens with long hours of that solitude, which they spend in contemplation and maybe even prayer. They live out where the buffalo and cell phone are both roaming, and that minimizes the noisy invasion of social and antisocial media. It gives a man time to think his own thoughts — deeper thoughts.

They read poetry. Some even write it — on the back of a label peeled off a can of beans. A lot of it is pretty funny, by the way. A little humor goes a long way in tough circumstances.

In my ever-growing mountain of books, right next to the writings and commentaries of the early Church Fathers, I have a collection of more than one hundred leather-bound western novels by my favorite storyteller of all time, Louis L'Amour. In fact, his last editor, Lou Aronica, was my first editor. L'Amour, more than anyone else, educated me on the life and philosophy of the cowboy. I urge men to read his books and young fathers to read them to their sons. You know, Jesus told stories more than He preached because He knew stories have a way of getting people's attention, bringing the point home with more clarity. Stories also remind us that, in a way, we're all *living* a story — an adventure story. Louis L'Amour's books, without preaching, just seem to seep into the soul and inspire men to ride the high ground.

L'Amour wrote much about the land, about the toughness of the Native Americans and the grit of the cowboys who went

West. The women in his books are almost always strong too—unlike the women in the books by authors before him. L'Amour researched his books by reading old newspapers, dime novels, and letters. He would talk with locals about their own recollections, the stories they had heard from their neighbors, and the challenges that they all faced.

He was a merchant marine by trade. He was also a boxer. More than anything else, he was a family man. From their home in Southern California, he would drive his wife, Katherine, and their kids in their station wagon on Route 66 and all over the West, which he would later write about. They would ride horses, hike, and explore the topography that would find its way into his books. They say that if there's a hill, a rock, a stream, or a tree mentioned in one of his novels, then, more likely than not, it's really out there somewhere. He and his books are as authentic as the cowboy.

You see, Louis L'Amour was raised in the tough environs of the Dakotas, where I was born. Believe me, life there is tough. I spent the first few years of my youth there until my parents moved us to the Monterey Bay area. I remember, as a boy living under the warm California sun, looking at a newspaper clipping of a man standing on a snowdrift in the Dakotas. The top of the telephone pole barely reached his waist.

The title of my TV and Prime Video series, *Long Ride Home with Bear Woznick*, was subconsciously based on the title of one of L'Amour's books. I did not realize that it was inspired by him until years later, when I was moving some of his books to a new bookshelf and a single book fell to the ground. I leaned down to pick it up, and there it was with the title just gleaming out in gold letters against the dark-brown leather cover: *Long Ride Home*. I learned a lot from that man, for encoded in his stories was the

Cowboy Code, which is actually a code of virtue; in turn, it was encoded into my soul.

The men in Louis L'Amour's books are not perfect, but they are defined by their resolute pursuit of virtue. Though they are strong—and, if need be, intimidating—they are humble and never make a person feel small—unless that person needs to be knocked down a peg or two.

The pack that rides with me on my TV show *Long Ride Home* has the same grit as the cowboys in Louis L'Amour's books, as well as that desire for solitude. Around every turn, there is an element of danger awaiting us as we adventure on roads we have never ridden before. We face heat, bitterly cold rain, and sometimes snow—and, of course, an onslaught of bugs hitting us like bullets.

When we saddle up, we have to have our wits about us. We are tuned in to the moment and on high alert for every movement, every crack in the pavement, every potential danger. At the same time, we are alive to the scenery, the smells and sounds of the road, in a way that only cowboys and bikers know. Though we are alive in the moment, our thoughts still wander in contemplation, searching the high ground of our souls like elk herding in the mountains in the fall.

Recently, I was speaking in Boise, Idaho—real cowboy country—for EWTN's Salt and Light Radio. Afterward, as I signed books, an older-looking man stood before me with his wife. I looked up at this tall, lithe man, shook his strong hand, and heard myself asking, "Are you a cowboy?"

With true cowboy humility, he answered, "Well, I have always worked on ranches."

His wife spoke up. "Yes. He is a cowboy." That is all that was said. But the next day, I saw them again. I had suggested to the radio station that we invite a few bikers to enjoy a short ride between events. When we got to the meetup spot, there were more than sixty bikers from Knights on Bikes, and our little three-hour ride became an eight-hour expedition along the Payette River. That cowboy and his wife from the night before had volunteered to ride sweep in the support truck, trailing us, carrying food and water, and standing by in case of a breakdown or an emergency.

As we pulled over next to the canyon stream for a midday break, it was so peaceful that it was hard to tell the difference between the sound of the breeze through the pines and the sound of the rushing rapids. Cindy and I sat down on a log for a respite, and we noticed that the cowboy and his wife sat on a bench nearby. We were drawn to them. I went over to them and asked her, "Are the men today anything like cowboys?"

"No," she bluntly replied. "Men today are not anything like cowboys." There was a whole book lingering in her response. (Actually, I guess you could say *this* is that book.) But she said no more. Her words hung there in my mind like an unlatched screen door banging in the wind in a lonely prairie cabin. Her words inspired in me a response, and to some degree that is what this book is.

I could sense the smallest bit of angst in her voice, but mostly there was just a real sense of loss. It was her honest response to an honest question—short and to the point, as cowboys and cowgirls are apt to be. She knew that we need our men today to return to the resilience, reliability, and humility of the cowboy.

So what was the Cowboy Way? Or should I say, what *is* the Cowboy Way? Because, as long as there are cattle, there will be cowboys riding the range.

Cowboys are perceptive and decisive. Part of their ease in making decisions comes from knowing what they stand for, and they know how to make a stand. They know what they believe, and they live by a personal Creed and the Cowboy Code. They are quick to act when needed. They are clever but not conniving. For them, it is simple to understand what needs to be done, even though the doing of it might not be easy.

When push comes to shove, they cannot be shoved. Their reputations precede them, and their good name is their most valuable possession. They are not quick to anger, but if someone calls them a liar, a cheat, or a thief, or disrespects a woman, or messes with their horse, that interloper is in for a world of hurt.

They believe in justice and in the rule of law. In their saddle bags, Louis L'amour's men carry hardtack, flour, beef jerky, bacon, beans, and coffee; usually they also pack a Bible, or Plato's *Republic,* or even a book on the law. They sleep with one eye open at night, alert for danger, and rise just before first light. Though there is a fire in their bellies, they are slow to anger. They know how to diffuse a conflict with a prideful man without fists or gunplay. Their words are few but pack a punch.

They can be trusted, and they give to each man what is due to him. They are prudent in pursuing their day's work and their life's goals. They are wise with their money. They pinch out savings when they can, and they keep the money in an old coffee can next to their gunpowder. Sometimes they invest in businesses as silent partners or buy a spread of land to start their own cattle ranch.

When it comes to running a ranch, they are skilled hands. They prefer to do their work while on their horse whenever possible. Have you ever seen a cowboy get off his horse to open a gate? No. They take care of things. They take even better care of animals and people. After a long ride, they water, feed, and rub down their horses before they take care of their own needs.

A cowboy's ranch is no rawhide outfit, hastily thrown together and then ignored, with fence posts leaning over and roofs patched together and things left unmended. They build things to last. They log the wood from the trees on their land and trim the logs for their cabins, barns, and corrals.

They keep their guns clean, reload them as soon as they are fired, and keep them always close by. As John Wayne says in one of his Westerns, "A rifle in the wagon is worthless."

Louis L'Amour's cowboy heroes are providers. They are protectors. Though they have a desire for women, you do not see them lusting after them. Most certainly, sex is for after marriage. L'Amour's cowboys respect women and carefully protect their honor. Though they are often slow in coming to love, when they do love a woman, they are all in. They step in between danger and the vulnerable.

They always travel light. They know where the next watering hole is and how to find a new one. They are alert and aware of their surroundings, whether in a crowded room or on a mountain trail. They are always watching their back trail for a stalking predator—whether man or beast. As they ride, they always look back, because the trail looks different when you are going out from when you are coming in. That's a good lesson for us now, when so many are rejecting our history. Remember that by looking back, you may just find your way forward.

They fiercely love their Mas and Pas, their aunts and uncles and cousins. They love even more fiercely their own woman and their children. They love their country. In a fight, they may not always win, but they never back down either. They have grit—a word we don't hear much of these days. They have fortitude. They press on in the toughest of circumstances on long trail drives or through deserts or snowstorms.

Where have all the cowboys gone?

A good man defines himself by the hardships he endures in facing and overcoming the challenges in his pursuit of his Creed and his mission. God stands by a man like this. "For the eyes of the LORD run to and fro throughout the whole earth, to give strong support to those whose heart is blameless toward him" (2 Chron. 16:9). A good man does not squander the gifts that God infused into his soul at that sacred moment of conception. The Lord gave him gifts and a unique calling to go along with them. A good man knows there is a job to be done, and he knows *he* is the man who can do it.

In the past, Satan pushed men to be macho, misogynistic, domineering jerks. Now, it seems, the devil's pendulum has swung the other way. Today, he sissifies and castrates men. Why? Because he hates men. He especially hates fathers, for the title of Father first and foremost belongs to the first Person of the Trinity. Hell is waging an all-out war on fathers and fatherhood. And if you look at society today, from the court system to pop culture, it sure does seem as if the devil is winning.

The devil desperately tries to cancel manliness because true manliness is godliness. He hates men because the second Person of the Trinity became one. The devil used to be called Lucifer ("light-bearer") when he was one of the highest of all the angels. He wanted to be God the Father. Instead, Jesus calls him the "father of lies" (John 8:44). A father procreates, but Satan is impotent. All he can do is try to destroy what is good.

A good man has a target on his back, but God stands with him. One man plus God is a majority. One man plus God wins. It is time for men to take a stand—to cowboy up.

In case you have not yet figured it out, Satan is a punk. St. Michael the Archangel and his armies defeated him and his demons and cast him out of Heaven. Then he had his head stomped on by a lowly handmaiden, who triumphed over him forever simply by saying "Yes, please" to God's will. (Will we have any less courage than Our Lady?)

Satan glorifies the metrosexual, porn-addicted, woke, genderless, sissified, self-seeking, glory-seeking, money-grubbing, atheistic, afraid-of-his-own-shadow, man-boy who won't get off the couch or out of his parents' basement, won't ask a girl out (may take her to bed but not marry her), has dogs instead of kids, has lots of toys, kind of a man-boy whose greatest virtue is to take offense at whatever the latest cancel culture dictates. Don't be that man-boy.

Society has enlisted in the devil's diabolical sissifying of men, marginalization of fathers, and culture canceling of families. "It takes a village to raise a child," they say. No. First and foremost, it takes a mom and a dad—a husband and a wife—to raise a child.

Our world has been pushed past the point of teetering on the edge of destruction. We are careening down the slippery slope. The neutered social justice warrior sees himself as a victim, demands that society take care of him, and spends more time looking in the mirror and primping his beard, his hair, and his clothes than looking into the empty chasm of his soul. His quest in life seems to be more about winning the latest video game than seeking worthy goals and challenges that require him to grow in virtue. His first thoughts are for his own comfort rather than a willingness to lay down his life to serve God and others. He thinks of what he can get instead of what he can give.

This man-boy victimizes women through his addiction to porn and "dating" (hookup) apps. He falls in an ever-inward, downward, Dante-like spiral as he fills himself with more and more emptiness; while victimizing women, he damages his soul with his porn addiction but does not save his virginity for that special woman he may someday meet and marry. If he ever gets married, he does not protect and cherish his woman. He sees her merely as a partner instead of a special gift whom he must put first and care for. God made man out of mud, but the woman is not made of mud: she is more highly refined, since God took her from man's rib (see Gen. 2:7, 21–22). She is to be honored, respected, protected, and cherished.

Today's man-boy measures his happiness by how many pistons he owns and how many toys he has. He has plenty of opinions, which he yells at the TV, but he never does anything about anything. He drops his kids off at soccer but does not coach the team. He rationalizes pursuing a career instead of balancing his time with his family.

That is not you. I get the feeling you're saddling up right now. You are just the man for a time such as this.

This book is a toolbox that should help you grow in wisdom and virtue. Let's be clear, though: this is not a self-help book. It is the farthest thing from that. I'm not going to lead you on one of those inward, downward spirals just to leave you in isolated self-obsession. This book calls you *outward* into servant leadership. It will help you to develop a sense of mission. We'll set goals, and we'll put your gifts to use toward achieving those goals. Never forget your highest calling: to love others responsibly — not in some general, empathetic, pathetic sense but in the blood and guts of laying down your life for the people in your life, most especially your family and your friends.

The Bible does not say, "God so loved the world that He felt all warm and gushy inside." He took action. He willed the true good through self-donation. "He gave His only Son, that whoever believes in him should not perish but have eternal life"

(John 3:16). This is what being a man is: laying down your life for those you love. It is to protect, to provide, to serve, to cherish by the will of the Lord in the service of God.

This book is a roundup of sorts, a long trail drive. If you sign up to ride with this outfit, it means that you are a man with the guts and determination to take on a challenge and better yourself. The trail changes a man. This one will too. You will not be the same at the end of this ride.

God is calling us to be as heroic as cowboys, so, as our tail gunner, Grady Dyke, calls out to the men when we are ready to roll thunder on our motorcycles on *Long Ride Home*, "Saddle up! Let's ride!"

Know Your Creed, Live by Your Code

A man's got to have a code—a creed he
can live by, no matter the job.

—John Wayne as Hondo Lane, in the film *Hondo*,
based on the novel by Louis L'Amour

Every man should know what he stands for, what his life is all
about, and what rules he will live by. Every man needs to define
his own personal Creed and then a Code of rules to pursue that
Creed. A Creed is a short thought, a pronouncement, a mission,
an overarching purpose. It states a man's deepest desire and thus
defines him. Your Code, when consistently applied to your life
choices, decisions, and actions, will help you reach that goal and
fulfill your Creed, your purpose.

Your Creed and your Code may evolve over the years as your
life experience, adventures, and misadventures take you deeper
into your core, into your guts, and you discover more and more
what you are made of—and what you are made *for*, what your
God-given gifts and desires draw you to. Be prepared to adjust
your Creed and your Code as you grow. Man writes in pencil;
God writes in stone tablets. He has a story, an adventure, planned

only for you and that only you can live out, and He has written it on your heart. He is "the author and finisher of our faith" (Heb. 12:2).

Adventure, by the way, is just another way of saying that, on your path, things can go wrong. To have lived a life of adventure means that we at times have bitten off more than we can chew, and we had to grow to accomplish it. In a way, that is a definition of a worthy goal. It means we have lived through some gnarly challenges and adversity in our pursuits — or that at times those things seem to pursue us. Our response to tough times shapes us. In fact, soft times can be the most dangerous of times as we easily drift into the backwater of mediocrity. But perhaps more so does our response to times of ease shape us. With our right response and friendship with God, He is able to make "all things work together for good" (Rom. 8:28).

Some say you can really get to know a man by seeing how he responds to adversity. To a degree, that is true, and most real men will rise to overcome that adversity. That's how you become a better man. In fact, this is the first step toward manhood. But perhaps even more challenging are the times when life is easy, when a man basks in prosperity and power. Does he squander that time and so become weaker? Honestly, that's how most of us seem to go through life today — especially when we think of how tough life was just a hundred years ago in the Old West.

A century ago, life was hard, work was dangerous, and life expectancy was short. Food on the table was not guaranteed. We consider times to be tough when we run out of soft, comfy toilet paper. Clean drinking water, air conditioning, and heat are taken for granted today and considered more of a right than a privilege. We can fly across the United States in five hours, whereas cowboys rode their wagons on a hazardous five-month expedition to go out west.

How are you responding to your relative prosperity? Do you squander your money and your leisure time? Or are you building something? Real men build. Lazy men complain and tear down. Are you building your inner man? Are you building up your wife, your children? Are you building up those around you? Are you pressing on to your high calling as a man made in God's image? Or are you getting lazy and weak—physically, mentally, and spiritually? Perhaps a man is made more for the storm at sea than for the peaceful harbor.

The prosperous man may start to think too highly of himself and lose touch with his roots. He may forget how hard life can be for those around him. Does he use his successes to peacock, to pursue more prestige and power and pride? St. Thomas Aquinas said that pride is the queen of all vices and vainglory her favorite child. Does the prosperous man get fat and lazy in his mind and in his body, squandering his wealth and squandering his time in the pursuit of emptiness, with a disordered desire for created things instead of the Creator? Does he trade the joy of cooperating with God on the deep adventure along the path that He lays out for us—of willing the true good for others and giving oneself to that cause—for Esau's bowl of porridge or, worse, hummus and kale?

The monks of the desert had a Creed that they lived by: *Memento mori*. This Creed was first used when it was spoken to victorious Roman generals as they made their triumphal entry into the city of Rome. As he rode in on his horse, without his army, in a parade of the plunder and the newly captured slaves—as the citizens, plebes, and the slaves of Rome cheered him as if he were a god—a lowly servant walked behind him, just within earshot, and repeated the words loud enough for the general to hear above the roaring crowds: "*Memento mori*." *Remember your death.*

It was meant to remind him, "Even with all that you have done, you are not all that." As they say in *Fight Club*, "You're not your job. You're not how much money you have in the bank. You're not the car you drive. You're not the contents of your wallet."

Both prosperity and adversity bring their challenges. Man must rise above both of them and live in his dignity and purpose. The monks of the desert knew this. Though they lived their lives in solitude, isolated in their individual caves, they would come together once a week or maybe once a month for Mass and common prayer. Their words to each other were few and spoken only when necessary. Their greeting to each other was simple; it was the Creed they lived by: "*Memento mori. Remember your death.*"

The monks did not repeat this Creed in some morbid way; rather, they saw it as a promise, as a hope of the bliss of Heaven and the Beatific Vision of God. We need to live remembering that we are going to die. We choose whether we go to Heaven or Hell. It is 100 percent under our control.

With just two Latin words, the desert monks summed up their purpose. Their small and large decisions, their devotion to prayer, and their every action were all based on that guiding thought.

So, consider: what is your purpose in life? Is the "hokey pokey" really what it's all about?

Here is my personal Creed: "The most radical quest you can pursue in life is to abandon yourself to the wild adventure of God's Will." Some of my Personal Code, the Rules that I seek to live by, you will find in the Rules in this book. I hope you will ponder them, as cowboys are known to do, and then write for yourself your own Creed and your own Code of Rules and then live by them.

As a Benedictine oblate, I made a vow to live by our Creed of stability, fidelity, and obedience. I pursue the way of life that was lived by St. Benedict, which he laid out in his "little rule for beginners"—that is, *The Holy Rule of Saint Benedict.* He wrote these rules for fifth-century monks, but that Code is still in use today by many orders of monks and nuns. You will find some elements of his rules in this book too.

So consider what your Creed is. My boyhood hero—lifeguard, surfer, Olympic champion, and "Ambassador of Aloha," Duke Kahanamoka—had a Creed: "In Hawaii we greet friends, loved ones, and strangers with *Aloha,* which means 'love.' … It is my Creed."

Our Queen Ke'opuolani spoke her Creed as she was baptized into the Christian Faith back in 1825, and it is now our Hawaiian state Creed: *Ua Mau ke Ea o ka 'Aina i ka Pono*—"The life of the land is perpetuated in righteousness."

King David of Israel had a Creed: "One thing have I asked of the LORD, that will I seek after: that I may dwell in the house of the LORD all the days of my life, to gaze upon the beauty of the LORD and to inquire in his temple" (Ps. 27:4). The Rules, the Code he sought to live by could be summed up in the Ten Commandments handed down to Moses by God.

On the right-hand corner of my desk, I have a small engraved plaque that reminds me daily of one Rule in my Code (that is, "Ride for the Brand"). It is based on the name of the desk in the Oval Office that first belonged to President Hayes. Hayes lived in the days of the burgeoning West—the days of the cowboys—after the Civil War. He named that desk "The Resolute." The plaque on the right front top of my desk is based on that. It reads: "RESOLUTE DESK—Thy Will Be Done."

Hayes's Code, in turn, is based on the Creed that Jesus lived by: "Thy will be done." And you could say that the Code of Rules Jesus taught in His sermon on the Mount is summed up in the Beatitudes.

12 Rules for Manliness

I remember the Creed that the nuns taught in the *Baltimore Catechism*. "Q. Why did God make you? A. God made me to know Him, to love Him, and to serve Him in this world, and to be happy with Him for ever in heaven."

You will often hear a cowboy sum up his thoughts by referring to the "Cowboy Code." Though, of course, there is no formal written Cowboy Code, it is understood that there is an unwritten law that a cowboy is held to and aspires to. Here is a synthesis of various Cowboy Codes that I have gathered over the years:

- Never shoot first, hit a smaller man, or take unfair advantage.
- Live each day with honesty and courage.
- Take pride in your work. Always do your best.
- Always finish what you start.
- Do what has to be done.
- Be tough but fair.
- When you make a promise, keep it.
- Ride for the brand.
- Talk less and say more.
- Remember, some things aren't for sale.
- Know where to draw the line.
- Have respect for everyone you meet, especially women.
- Be gentle with children, the elderly, and animals.
- Be confident in your dreams.
- Stand up for what is right.
- Be a good steward of the land and its animals.
- Put the welfare of your family above your own.
- Go the distance.
- Help the vulnerable and those in distress.
- Keep clean in thought, word, and deed.

You cowgirls out there, look for a good man to marry who lives by that Code. Be sure to live by your own Code and you will have a good life. Here's an example:

- Dare to be a real cowgirl.
- Buck the rules. (I would add: break the ones that need to be broken, and do it elegantly. Christians in this day of paganism must do so.)
- Stay balanced in the saddle.
- Ride the trail of adventure.
- Dream as big as Texas.
- Be tough but feminine.
- Attack life like a thousand-pound steer.
- Saddle your own horse.
- Reign in your fears.
- Dress for success, the cowgirl way.
- Ride high in the saddle, but stay grounded.
- Give others a leg up.
- Always get back on the horse.
- Ride beside your man.
- Recharge your cowgirl spirit.
- Die with your boots on.

As a youth I proudly wore my Boy Scout uniform to school once a week. The Boy Scouts summarize their Creed in their oath: "On my honor I will do my best to do my duty to God and my country and to obey the Scout Law; to help other people at all times; to keep myself physically strong, mentally awake, and morally straight." Their Code had twelve rules. A scout is:

1. Trustworthy
2. Loyal
3. Helpful
4. Friendly

5. Courteous
6. Kind
7. Obedient
8. Cheerful
9. Thrifty
10. Brave
11. Clean
12. Reverent toward God

Bikers live by a code too. That is why bikers are some of the best people I know. There is a certain camaraderie that is bred from facing the common danger and the harsh elements of the road — the sense of adventure and long hours of solitude. There is especially a heightened sense of alertness and commitment to each other and to the Code when riding in a pack and the road captain yells "Kickstands up!" The following list sums up some of the elements of that code.

1. Family first: this includes the biker brotherhood.
2. No nonsense: give respect where it is due but expect respect from others.
3. Honor the bike: maintain your bike as you would a horse, and do not touch someone else's bike; that would be like touching his woman.
4. Never give up: set your mind on the job; then do it.
5. No rider left behind: hit the brakes when you see another biker in trouble.
6. Stay true to yourself: take responsibility for your actions.
7. Stick to your guns: keep your word; when push comes to shove, stand your ground.
8. Ride with the right gear: don't be a SQUID (stupid, quick, underdressed, imminently dead).

9. Ride with attentiveness and skill. Biking is a learned skill coupled with attentiveness, decisiveness, and courage.

10. Bonus code: Keep the rubber side down.

I used to go into prisons and lead Bible studies. The convicts there have a code that we could all learn something from. It can be summed up simply as this:

> I am responsible for everything I say and do. If I break the rules, I am responsible. If I get caught with contraband, it isn't the fault of the person who sold it to me; I am responsible. If someone has a beef with me, it's not for me to talk with others about it. I need to go right to the one complaining, deal with it, and, if I am wrong, make it right.

I am a ninja black belt. Our ancient Creed is represented by the ancient ninja logo that is worn over the heart on our gi. It means, "Though my enemy hold his sword to my heart, I will prevail." The Code we sought to live by was codified by my teacher Master Stephen Hayes as a "Code of Protector Ethics":

- I protect life and health.
- I avoid violence whenever possible.
- I respect the property and space of all.
- I avoid taking what has not been offered.
- I develop significant relationships.
- I avoid abusing others for selfish pleasure.
- I thoughtfully express the truth.
- I avoid the confusion of dishonest words.
- I cultivate a positive attitude, a healthy body, and a clear mind.
- I avoid whatever would reduce my physical or mental well-being.

- I communicate health, happiness, and peace of mind to everyone I meet.
- I avoid violent, disturbing, and unduly critical speech.
- I promote harmony and positive momentum to bring out the best in everyone.
- I avoid causing alienation, doubt, and division among others.
- I encourage all to speak purposefully from the heart.
- I avoid the dull contentment of gossip and small talk.
- I am as enthusiastic about others' fulfillment as I am about my own.
- I avoid treating others' successes as the cause of my lacks.
- I promote the enjoyment of life and encourage others with my smile.
- I avoid setting myself against the world.
- I strive for the personal realization of truth.
- I accomplish what must be done in a timely and effective way.
- I avoid putting off what will benefit me and my world today.
- I strive to be so strong that nothing can disturb my peace of mind.
- I avoid the negative effects of worry, doubt, and regret.
- I work to build love, happiness, and loyalty among all members of my family.
- I avoid putting temporary personal benefit ahead of the welfare of those I love.

The Marines have a very simple Creed. It is simple but not easy: *Semper fi*—"Always faithful." They have a Code, too:

1. Never lie.
2. Never cheat or steal.

3. Abide by an uncompromising code of integrity.
4. Respect human dignity and respect others.
5. Honor compels Marines to act responsibly, to fulfill our obligations, and to hold ourselves and others accountable for every action.

Two thousand five hundred years ago, Socrates had a Creed summed up by his student Plato in these words: "We cannot live better than in seeking to become better.... The unexamined life is not worth living.... Know thyself." His Code was the pursuit of the four cardinal virtues:

> Prudence
> Temperance
> Justice
> Fortitude

So what is your Creed? What are the rules of your Code? What are your Rules for Manliness? What is it you stand for? What is your Standard? As the mounted cavalry rode into battle, they arrayed themselves in battalions, and each battalion had its own flag (or, as they called it, a standard). In the confusion of battle, the Standard was their rallying point, and more than that, the general observing the battle could see just where his different battalions were and how to deploy them.

Can you do the same? What are the Standards you rally to? Remember: how you do anything—even the littlest of things—is how you do everything. What Rules do you deploy and live by in the heat of battle, in your pursuit of your Creed, on your quest for a victorious and virtuous life? As St. Paul said, "I have fought the good fight, I have finished the race" (2 Tim. 4:7).

Take time now to think that through and write a first draft, in a sentence or two, that states your Creed—what your life quest is. Craft your own words. Be sure that every word is powerful.

Then, over the days ahead, as you ponder and read this book, let it read you. Refine that Creed and then begin to carefully craft your own Code of Rules that you will live by and that you will hand down and teach to your sons and daughters, both in your words and your deeds.

One very important point: in your Creed and your Code do not use the word *try* because, as John Wayne said, "Trying don't get the job done, son."

A knife is sharpened by stone, steel is tempered by fire, but men must be sharpened by men.

—Louis L'Amour, *The Walking Drum*

Rule 2

Ride for the Brand

I've covered a lot of territory in my time,
but when I take a man's money,
I ride for the brand.

— Louis L'Amour, *Conagher*

When a cowboy agrees to take a man's wages to ride for him, it goes without saying that he will be loyal to that man's outfit. If the cowboy loses respect for the ranch he has signed on to, he is free to collect his wages and leave, but as long as he rides for that outfit, his loyalty is expected, and he gives it.

Cowboys are a loyal breed. Come hell or high water, a cowboy rides for the brand. Though the cowboy knows no man as his master, once he gives his word to be hired on with a ranch, the boss and the other hands expect that cowboy to be as diligent about his work as they are. People know who a cowboy rides for. Do people know who you ride for?

Long before Wall Street developed "brand marketing," cowboys claimed ownership of their horses or cattle by branding them with a hot iron. Usually the brand is a variation of a letter with a symbol for some descriptive word, such as *lazy, walking, rocking, flying,* or *running,* as in the Flying V, the Rocking Triangle T, or the Lazy X.

Near Glacier Park, Montana, where I built a small, one-room hunter's cabin with the help of my sons and daughter, we found that, in most cases, a ranch's name and brand were boldly announced on a long log suspended over the entrance to the ranch by other large logs. Even a small ranch has a big sign. There can be no doubt whose range you are entering. Its gate, its horses, and its cattle all wear that same brand.

When people see you, do they know whose range they are on? Do they know who you ride for? God has a big spread. In fact, Scripture says that all the cattle on a thousand hills belong to Him. That's the brand I want to ride for. Do you?

God's brand has been handed down for generations. Two of the most ancient Christian brands are the Cross and the Fish. The Greek word for "fish" is *ichthys.* The early Christians used that word as an acronym for *Iesous Christos Theou Yios Soter:* "Jesus Christ, Son of God, Savior."

During the Early Church era—a time of deadly persecution, when a Christian met another person who he thought might be a Christian—he would casually scrape an arc in the dirt or on a tile. If the other person was a Christian, he would make an opposite intersecting arc to form a fish. They recognized each other as being Christians—that they both "rode for the brand." The same was done with the two lines of the cross.

What does it mean for a cowboy to ride for the brand? A cowboy rides long, lonely stretches in freezing rain and snow or sweltering heat and dust, always tending to his horse and the herd before he worries about himself. He often camps along the way. A cowboy always stubbornly prefers do his work in his saddle. Yet he still does what needs to be done, even if it has to be done on his feet. If being loyal to the brand means riding fence in the middle of freezing snow and rain, then so be it. Digging fence-post holes and repairing and stringing barbed wire that cuts him right through his leather gloves is as much a part of his job as settling the cows down at sunset as he sings to them.

The hazards of flash floods or lightning or his horse breaking a leg is not made up for by the romantic notion of sleeping under the stars because that often means sleeping under a slicker on a wet bed roll in a driving rain. At times, the cowboy has to fight off predators, such as wolves, mountain lions, bears, or even rustlers.

Who do you ride for? If it is only for yourself and your selfish pursuits, I pity you. You are missing out on a great adventure, and worse, you are living in a slow, inward, downward spiral into isolation from others, from God, and from your true self. A cowboy was made to ride the wild, wide-open range with God, and so are you.

As we ride for the brand in friendship with God, we find that we understand more and more His intentions, His plans, and His heart for us, for our families and friends, and for the world. We are not wage slaves. We are not just hired hands who serve God because of what we hope He will do for us or out of fear of what He will do if we don't serve Him. In time, our service draws us into a friendship with God. Jesus said it like this: "No longer do I call you servants, for the servant does not know what his master is doing; but I have called you friends" (John 15:15).

Jesus also says this about riding for the brand: "You are my friends if you do what I command you" (John 15:14). In time, we come to know and trust that His commands all have the best possible intentions for us and others, so we stop clinging to our saddle horn. We learn to "let go and let God."

Do we ride for the brand because we have a warm place to bunk in the winter and good grub as we herd the Lord's cattle? Or do we serve God because our heart compels us to? Are we committed to the Lord? More importantly, are we devoted to Him with a heart to serve Him and to please Him? Is our love a mercenary love that trades obedience for His consolations and hoped-for heavenly reward, or is our love a complete emptying of self? Do we desire only to know the Lord and to make Him known—that is, to love others not just for their sakes and not just for our sakes but, rather, for God's sake? "Peter, if you love me feed my sheep" (see John 21:17). Do you love God back? Do you love Him enough to will the true good and act on that good for others?

When you can, ride for a brand. Work for a company and a boss that have integrity. But above all, become a leader yourself—and one who has integrity, for that is the number-one quality that draws people to a leader. Integrity means leading a life with a singleness of purpose. A man who leads a double life is only fooling himself.

Every man must take stock of himself and realize that, in some way or another, he is a leader; you do not know who is watching you, learning from you—in a sense, following you. The only question is: Where are you leading people *to*?

My dad taught me, before I started my first job out of college, that I should write a philosophy of how I would approach that job. His sage advice stressed that my first statement in that philosophy should be to help my boss to be successful. I have worked around very brilliant and talented men, but their focus was their own ambition instead of the success of the company they worked for. They did not ride for the brand. Back in the days of ancient Rome, to be ambitious was considered a vice, not a virtue. The Latin root for *ambition* means to make a circle—to go around, as in behind someone's back. Being clever and conniving and taking shortcuts for your own end is not a virtue; it's being a snake in the grass. I have come upon rattlers hiding out in deep grass more than once. They are a scourge to a man on foot or in the saddle. I have learned to stay on the trail whenever possible.

Honorable men must take the straight path of virtue and service. It is this path that leads us to wide-open vistas. Advancement, then, comes to us as a byproduct of our service and loyalty, not through conniving cleverness and selfishness. "Work heartily, as for the Lord and not for men, knowing that from the Lord you will receive the inheritance as your reward" (Col. 3:23-24).

Do you seek promotion? The Bible says it straight out, without pulling any punches; "Promotion comes from the Lord."[2] Instead, be "faithful in small things and he will give you charge over greater."[3] In other words, ride for the brand. This is the true path toward your purpose and calling.

As you are placed in positions of leadership, the loyalty of the people who work for you does not come from higher wages, corporate bonding retreats, or a benefits package. It is earned by you through one thing: integrity. Dedication to your company, your boss, and your staff are important, but above that must be your dedication to your own Creed and Code. My dad taught me that being a professional and having integrity means doing the right thing even when no one else is looking.

Who was the man that Jesus said had more faith than anyone in all of Israel? (Hint: this man was not even Jewish.) A

---

[2] See Psalm 75:6-7: "For not from the east or from the west / and not from the wilderness comes lifting up, / but it is God who executes judgment, putting down one and lifting up another."

[3] See Matt. 25:21: "You have been faithful over a little; I will set you over much."

Roman centurion approached Jesus one day and asked Him to heal his servant. Being a centurion meant that he was a man under obedience to a commander. He, in turn, had one hundred men in his charge. Listen to what this man said about riding for the brand:

When Jesus said He would come to heal his servant, which would have meant traveling a very long distance, the centurion responded, "Lord, I am not worthy to have you come under my roof, but only say the word, and my servant will be healed." Notice first that he came to Jesus out of concern for one of those he had authority over. He was being loyal to his servant by seeking help for him.

Then he went on to say these profound words: "For I too am a man under authority." Do you see? He respects authority in his own life and is riding for the brand. Then he goes on to make the point that because he is loyal and respects authority, those under him do so too. "And I say to one, 'Go,' and he goes, and to another, 'Come,' and he comes, and to my servant, 'Do this,' and he does it" (see Matt. 8:5–13).

Jesus understood this, for He Himself lived by that Creed directed to His Father: "Thy will be done." He even submitted to Mary and Joseph. The Scripture says that, after they found Jesus in the Temple, "he went down with them and came to Nazareth and was submissive to them.... And Jesus increased in wisdom and in stature and in favor with God and man"(Luke 2:51–52). For this reason He submitted to death, even to death on the Cross, and so all authority has been given to Him, both in Heaven and on earth (see Matt. 28:18). The key to having authority is to ride for the brand.

And so the Centurion gives his loyalty to Jesus and expresses his faith in Him: "Only say the word, and my servant will be healed." The centurion understood authority when he saw it. He knew Jesus had authority over everything, and he put his faith in Him.

Riding for the brand means respecting authority. It is in respecting authority that the spiritual battle line is drawn and the fight against the powers of darkness is won.

Jesus affirms that a man who respects earthly authority in his life has a better grasp of God's authority in His Kingdom. It is Satan who led the failed rebellion in Heaven.

The devil hates and fears God's authority. That is why, during a tough exorcism or demonic encounter, even a Protestant pastor knows to call in reinforcements. He knows to call in a Catholic priest. Why is a Catholic exorcist so effective against demons? Because there is an apostolic lineage of God-given authority in the Catholic bishops and priests that is handed down by the laying on of hands in a direct line back to the primitive Church and even to the apostles, in fact, all the way back to Jesus. Talk about authority! Each bishop, each priest, each Catholic has been baptized by someone who was, in turn, baptized by someone in a long line all the way back to Jesus.

The bishop of each diocese appoints an exorcist who is under the bishop's God-given apostolic authority. Just as the kings in the Old Testament did when they appointed prime ministers and gave them their keys, their seals, and the authority to bind and loose, Jesus gave this binding and loosing authority to Peter and the other apostles. The apostles then went on to appoint others as bishops, and they, in turn, have appointed others over the centuries.

Demons tremble at the sound of Christ's Name, most especially when it is spoken by someone who is under authority—who is riding for the brand.

A man must demonstrate to his wife and family that he is under God's authority. They need to see that the father is riding for the brand. Then they, in turn, will respect the father's servant leadership.

Before Saul became the first king of Israel, his job was to drive stubborn mules. He had to push them and force them to do his will. He ran his kingdom the same way, with force and intimidation. This is how the devil tries to run his demonic kingdom, along with his human minions. Just look at the cancel culture. There is no leadership there: just a circular firing squad forcing its own will through bullying and intimidation upon anyone that it can eventually destroy. You can recognize that the devil is at work there because he is the original bully, and, like most bullies, he is a punk.

If you ride for the brand, do not let anyone silence or intimidate you. Stand up and stand for Jesus and those you love and are called to serve.

The second king of Israel was David. He was a shepherd. A shepherd does not force his sheep: rather, he leads them by his voice. If one lags behind, the shepherd goes to find him and bring him back. After the noontime gathering of all the sheep and all the shepherds at the watering hole, all it takes is for the shepherd to call out, and his flock separates from the other flocks and follows him. This is how David led Israel. His people's loyalty to him was profoundly responsive—that is, until he began to lose his integrity and, in so doing, lost their devotion.

Even the pope is referred to as "the servant of the servants of God." Authority does not mean to lord it over others but to serve. Authority—true authority, the type that people easily give allegiance to—leads by example, for the good of all. Think of a general who leads the charge into battle. He leads from the front. Do this for your family and for your friends. Lead from the front.

Cowboys have to work a bit to get cattle up and moving in the same direction. Once the cattle are moving, though, they just follow the cowboys in front of them. The cowboys are there to take care of them, to keep them healthy on good grass and grain, and to guide them—all part of riding for the brand.

If you ride for the brand in all the small decisions and challenges of your life, you will prove to be not only God's servant but His trusted friend and companion. In revealing His plans to you, He will show you not only the *what* but the *why*. He will ride along beside you and you will truly get to know Him and become His friend.

Trail dust is thicker than blood.

—Louis L'Amour, *The Daybreakers*

Rule 3

Be a Man of Your Word

*I learned a long time ago that a name is
only what a person makes it.*

— Louis L'Amour, *Lonely on the Mountain*

A cowboy's word is his bond. He makes a good name for himself
by keeping his promises. In fact, how can he really be called a
man if he is not a man of his word? A good name, to a cowboy,
is most highly valued.

Jesus Christ made it perfectly clear: "Let your yes mean yes
and your no mean no" (see Matt. 5:37).

A cowboy's contract with another man was bound by his
looking the other man in the eye and simply shaking his hand.
Deeds to horses or cattle were signed over, but that was not for
the sake of that buyer or seller. It was merely a tag of legal ownership for future transactions and to avoid future accusations of
rustling from others.

The cowboy's word meant that he could be counted on to tell
the truth, not mince words, and to shoot straight. He would say
what needed to be said, when it needed to be said, to whom—and
only to whom—it needed to be said. It meant that when he made

a promise, he made a commitment, whether that was to get a job done or maintain a secret trust. He stuck to it, come hell or high water. You could count on a cowboy's word, and often that was a matter of life and death. In a cowboy's world, his failure to keep his promise to watch over cattle or to herd horses or to stand guard could mean not only a financial loss: it could mean a loss of life.

Once a man breaks his word, he can never really gain that broken trust back. Your word will be doubted perhaps for the rest of your life. The Acts of the Apostles tells us that Paul and Barnabas had a great falling out and even parted ways over a dispute as to whether to trust the young John Mark, who had not kept his word, to stay with them on their dangerous and rigorous missionary trip. He abandoned them when times got tough (15:36–40).

John Mark went on to travel with Barnabas, whose name means "son of encouragement" (Acts 4:36). Barnabas encouraged and strengthened John Mark. He manned up and wound up being a great help to him. In time, that young man assisted Peter in Rome and wrote the Gospel of Mark.

There is a lesson to be learned from this. Do not easily trust a man who has broken his word to you. (I mean that. Hang on to this warning.) But then, if you *do* give him a second chance—and maybe we all do need that chance for redemption—encourage him to be a man of his word. Still, inspect what you expect from him.

As John Wayne said, "Every man deserves a second chance, but keep a strong eye on him." The world needs men, right now, to be cowboys. The world needs men who keep their word—and, more than that, who keep God's Word. If you have broken your word, do your best, even now, to go back and make it right to the extent that you can.

Probably one of the lowest things a man can do, by the way, is to break his word to a kid. Never break your word to a kid. Not only can it break his heart, but it teaches him not to trust—and not to be trustworthy. If you have broken a promise to a child, stop reading now and, to the best of your ability, go fix it. Did you promise to take your son fishing, or to coach his little league team? Did you promise your daughter to have a tea party with her, or to teach her how to bat? Even if your kids are adults, you can still find a way to keep your promise. The kid inside them needs and deserves that much from you. Earn that right to be called Father. Redemption, right? A second chance—even for you, right?

Our heavenly Father keeps His word. "Am I a man that I should lie?" He asks us (see Num. 23:19). On the contrary, "all the promises of God find their Yes in him. That is why it is through him that we utter our Amen to God for his glory" (2 Cor. 1:20). In other words, God is a man of His word.

On the other hand, Jesus called out the devil when He said, "Satan is a liar and the father of lies. He was a liar from the beginning" (see John 8:44). Jesus accused the religious leaders of His day, who twisted God's word to serve their own ends, as being the sons of this liar. That's a strong line. Which side do you stand on? Are you a man of your word?

Because a cowboy would rather die than break a promise, before he gives his word, he takes the full measure of the situation. In Larry McMurtry's book *Lonesome Dove*, Woodrow Call promises Gus McCrae that he would return Gus's body from Montana all the way back over a thousand miles to his beloved ranch in Rio Grande, Texas. Woodrow risked life and limb crossing prairies, deserts, mountains, and streams, but he brought his friend's body back to that place he loved. Keeping his word cost him a full year of his life and nearly cost him his life.

Words are a big deal. The second Person of the Trinity, Jesus, is called "the Word." John said, "In the beginning was the Word, and the Word was with God, and the Word was God.... All things were made through him, and without him was not any thing made that was made" (John 1:1, 3). Contemplate that for a moment. Just how powerful and important is a word? Almost fourteen billion years ago, God spoke the ontological words "Let there be light," and the universe was created. So began the chain of events that would lead to your being alive; you will live forever, after this life, either in Heaven or in Hell. You were shot like an arrow at that "Big Bang" moment from the heart of God across time and space.

Words are powerful. They can create or destroy.

Words are where the battle line is drawn. In the desert, your enemy, Satan, twisted Scripture to tempt Jesus, but Jesus battled him with the words of Scripture and defeated him. All of Satan's promises are meant only to bring you into his eternal bondage. He is a horse thief, a cattle rustler. He destroys crops and lands. He never builds. He cannot create. He is the snake in the grass. He cannot build up. He only destroys.

His words are only seeds for weeds. Don't let him plant his lies in your heart and mind—especially the ones that say you are not worthy of God's love or that God's promise of adventure for you is a lie. God considers you of incomparable worth. After all, He became a human Himself and gave His life to save you. Jesus took on our humanity to restore our dignity and to expose Satan's lie. The only seeds Satan carries are the seeds of his own destruction. For he cannot build. He can only tear down. He is the locust. He is the fire in the field.

Jesus cast Satan out "by the finger of God" (Luke 11:20), as a man flicks a fly off his shirt. Jesus cast out demons with just His words. He healed the blind and raised the dead with His words. He brought hope with His words. So don't despair: if He created the whole universe with His word, He can create a new heart in you. He can set you on His path of adventure that is meant just for you. He says, "I know the plans I have for you … plans for welfare and not for evil, to give you a future and a hope…. You will seek me and find me, when you seek me with all your heart"(Jer. 29:11, 13).

To be a man of your word, it helps to first be a man "of the Word."

As we can see, all of Scripture attests to the fact that words are powerful. So measure each word that you say. Is it true? Will you fulfill the promise you are considering making?

One of the biggest acts of cowardice is not to speak when remaining silent is a lie of acquiescence to a falsehood. Not saying what needs to be said to someone when it needs to be said is a lie by omission. "To make an apt answer is a joy to a man, and a word in season, how good it is!" (Prov. 15:23).

And what about the promises you have made to yourself? What words of commitment have you made to yourself that you have neglected? How many seemingly small promises have you made to yourself that you did not have the gumption to follow through on?

Writing down your Creed and your Code and seeking God's grace will propel you into a life of virtue and into transforming your dreams into goals and your goals into reality. Writing it down makes it a contract with yourself and an agreement with God — "according to Your will, God." Be sure to sign your Creed and your Code at the end and commit it to God to provide you the wisdom and grace to live it out.

Do you want to be the man your family and the world needs? Then be a man of truth. Be a straight shooter. Be a man whose word people can rely on.

The author of *The Lord of the Rings*, J. R. R. Tolkien, was a philologist, a historian of words. He taught English literature at Oxford and even made major contributions to the *Oxford Dictionary*. He taught that each word has a whole developmental history. Within each word, there is a story and a meaning, and to twist the use of that word is to pervert our heritage, which, in turn, perverts our trajectory as a people and distorts our understanding of our purpose. One of Tolkien's best friends, C. S. Lewis, was a linguist. He also warned of the degradation and dilution of the power of words.

Be precise and accurate in your word use. Don't tolerate the misuse of words by the woke mob. The twisting of words, which these two great friends warned us about, is one of the tools that Satan uses to unleash his chaos in our society. The fallen world—like its father, the devil—has co-opted and twisted the meaning of words. For example, the word *masculinity* was not meant to be a word that drifts along some gender spectrum. That is why I dropped it from my vocabulary. It has no meaning anymore. I just use the word *manliness*.

The fallen world twists and deforms words. Instead of referring to abortion as the murder of an unborn baby, the fallen world calls it "planned parenthood." Politicians give their legislation names that distort and hide their true purposes. When words are twisted this much, they make communication impossible. Confusion and chaos reign.

As during the French Revolution and the communist takeover of Eastern Europe, and like Haman and his sons in the book of Esther, the bullies of cancel culture will ultimately wind up hanging from their own gallows. Satan has no loyalty to his minions. The culture of death carries the seeds of its own destruction.

When Pilate questioned Jesus before His Crucifixion, he asked Him sarcastically, *"Quid est veritas?"* "What is truth?" (John 18:38). But Truth is a person, and He was standing right before Pilate. For Jesus said, "I am the Way, and the Truth and the Life. No one comes to the Father except through me" (John 14:6).

Speak the truth. Keep your word. Be a man of your word.

He was the kind if you got in trouble
you didn't look to see if he was still with
you—you knew damned well he was.

—Louis L'Amour, *Sackett*

Rule 4

Be Dangerous: Make a Stand

"I saw him and I liked what I saw, a very dangerous man but a man,
and I had a feeling if he gave his word it would prove good."

"You gave him something that meant more than anything else
could. You trusted him and you respected him. His kind of man wants
little else."

—Louis L'Amour, *Comstock Lode*

I personally know a dangerous man like the one Louis L'Amour mentions in the passage above. This man did not wait for trouble to come to Him. He went out looking for the biggest bully on the block. He first faced him down out in the desert—as in the Old West, where a lot of shootouts took place.

When He would walk through His enemy's turf, the devil's gang members, wildly afraid, would freak out and shriek, "What do we have to do with You, O Jesus, Son of David? Have you come to torment us?" And He would rebuke them, saying, "Gag yourself" (see Matt. 8:29; Mark 5:7; 1:25). And they did. But in time, the assaults became physical and violent. At one point, a rowdy mob even tried to throw Jesus off a cliff, but the Cosmic Cowboy didn't lose His cool. He didn't run and hide. In fact,

He simply walked through the crowd and went on His way. Not even Clint Eastwood is that cool.

As things began to come to a head, He found it useful one day to wield a whip. You know, there is a certain skill involved in using a whip. The untrained can hurt themselves worse than they hurt their targets. Jesus knew how to use a whip. He strode into the temple entryway and shouted, "My Father's house is meant to be a house of prayer, but you have made my Father's house a den of thieves!" He cracked His whip, kicked over chairs, threw over tables, and scattered the money (see Matt. 21:12–13).

Jesus was a dangerous man.

He was tough. As everyone would soon find out, He was tough as nails. You see, He had been trained up as a *tecknon*, as the Scripture says in Greek. The word means "builder." Now, there is not a lot of wooded area in Palestine—but there is a lot of limestone rock. Jesus probably worked in stone, and His sinews and muscles would have shown this. He grew strong as He worked to quarry and carve out stone bricks and then make walls with them. He was strong, and His hands were calloused. And just as He could eye up the straightness of a wall, He could size up the measure of a man.

Jesus was known to have said, "Do not think that I have come to bring peace to the earth. I have not come to bring peace, but a sword" (Matt. 10:34). And he drew a very clear line in the sand when He declared, "Whoever is not with me is against me" (Matt. 12:30). It had been said of Him in His youth that He "would be the cause of "the fall and rising of many" (Luke 2:34). And so He was. He was gnarly. He was dangerous. His very presence forced a response to His question "Who do you say that I am?" (Matt. 16:15). He was a threat to those who had "been weighed in the balances and found wanting" (Dan. 5:27). And they knew it.

At the age of thirty-three, He came to His final showdown with His archenemy.

The cry went out through the city, bustling with tourists all looking for a thrill and something to tell their neighbors about when they returned home. The man who had been cheered as the Messiah by the crowd only a week earlier was now jeered at by the same mob. "I saw it. I was there. I got the T-shirt."

It was "go time." Armed crowd control pushed and shoved the mob as they pressed and pushed closer to see. The fight that would turn the page of history, the fight of the centuries, was on. The guards held back the crowd, but they could not hold back the sickly, stinking flow of slithering demons that oozed a molten flow of fear and hate, lust for power, and jaundiced obscenity.

But it turns out that Jesus had staged this fight with His ancient enemy. Better said, He set him up. Satan's weapon is death. Jesus was determined to disarm him and slay His enemy with his own weapon.

As a black belt in the lethal ninja martial art, I am trained not just to attack and counterattack. I am trained to stage the fight. One of my favorite elements in training is knife fighting. The good news in a knife fight is that you pretty much know where the attack is coming from. It's coming from the hand with the knife.

You stage the fight by setting up a trap for your opponent by giving him an opening. Instead of trying to protect every area of your body and bobbing and weaving, you actually give your opponent an opening, knowing that he will most likely strike at the target you are presenting to him. He will see you as vulnerable there. When the attack comes, your response is immediate and effective, using his own energy and his own weapon to kill him.

I demonstrated this once at a Catholic men's conference with a friend of mine. He wielded a harmless wooden training knife.

I gave him a vulnerable target, so he instinctively sought to stab me there. As the stab came in, I "passed the knife" and then, using a subtle wrist throw, redirected the force of his arm and the knife; by my so doing, he slit his throat with his own knife as he went tumbling head over heels to the ground and into a submission hold. It happened so fast that he did not even know how he ended up on the ground.

Jesus staged a fight as well. Things were on a fast collision course with the enemies that He had made among the greedy and the power hungry as well as Satan and his gang of demons. Nothing could stop the coming showdown. But Jesus chose the time — "the fullness of time" (Gal. 4:4) — and He chose the place: Golgotha, meaning "the place of the skull" (John 15:22), the very place where Abraham offered up Isaac. This would be mortal combat, a fight to the end.

The battle raged over a night and a day, starting near an olive press and ending up on the opposite hill. At least, His enemy thought that it had ended.

For a while, it seemed as if Jesus was whipped. Finally, He fell, mortally wounded — but, in doing so, He took the blade of sin and death out of Satan's hand and slew him with it by rising from the dead. "Dying, He destroyed our death. Rising, He restored our life." The devil continues to rage, but he knows that he has been defeated and that Jesus is the champion. The devil lost. The Bible refers to him as the great dragon but also the "fleeing" dragon (see Isa. 27:1). He is defeated. He may try to wreak havoc with his sweeping tail as he runs, but, sure enough, he is fleeing.

I have been to the scene of this fight. I have been to the tomb where the Champion lay for three days. The only way you can reach inside is by getting down on your hands and knees, humbling yourself, and leaning way in through the narrow opening. This is the narrow gate we, too, must enter with humility.

Will you walk this dangerous way with Jesus? Not many of His men did that day. Yet Jesus is calling you to be just such a man, to be dangerous. "Be watchful, stand firm in the faith, act like men, be strong" (1 Cor. 16:13).

Jesus is calling you to pray that most dangerous prayer with Him to the Father: "Thy will be done."

Have you ever had someone introduce you as "a really nice guy"? Doesn't that just make you feel like a passive softy? It makes me want to throw up.

When I am introduced like that, I emphatically insist, "No, I'm not!" I hold back the gag reflex as the image of the Simpsons' neighbor Ned Flanders flashes through my mind. Or I think of the GIF of Homer retreating backward into a shrub so as not to be noticed. "I am the farthest thing from a nice guy. I want to be a good man. But I am not a nice guy."

Nice guys sit passively in the church pew. They vent with passive-aggressive behavior but never really confront anyone or anything. They seem like fine Christian men, but they are just man-boys. They remind me of those life-size cutout posters that the restaurants used to fill up the empty seats during COVID for the sake of social distancing. They have been social-distancing themselves since long before COVID, never wanting to get involved in the hard work of making an impact, of making a difference in their world. They are spectators in the stands, not combatants on the field, as they apologize for being born with a male appendage.

Nice guys like to think of themselves as society's victims, blaming others for their own mediocrity and malaise and the castration of their souls. Their mommies and daddies made life easy for them, congratulating them for their participation trophy, but Paul exhorts us to be champions, to "win the race" (1 Cor. 9:24).

As the world tries to marginalize men, we can't allow ourselves to be victims—to let the world run us over. It is each man's responsibility not to yield to society's desire to coddle and cuddle them, to cancel them, and to cuff them into that safe, passive place of mediocrity. A life half lived is a life not lived at all. There is no joy where there is no *telos*—no purpose. They say there is no need to be tough, gritty, and self-reliant. Yet the extent that you yield to the temptation of the safety net is the extent to which you lose your freedom. When a man yields his manhood to self-pity, he is basically telling God, "You failed me," and in so doing, he turns his back on God's will.

Nice guys take offense at every little thing, but if you are dangerous, you know that "love does not take offense" (see 1 Cor. 13:5). It tests everything and holds to what is good (see 1 Thess. 5:21). You boldly love back while staying the course with your Creed and your Code.

It's time for each man to stand up and be counted, to stand for something, to lead by example, to join with other men in the arena and fight for what is right.

The spirit of lawlessness is running amok in a fatherless world of men who have relegated themselves to the sidelines. Thugs, thieves, and vagrants abuse other peoples' rights as they take over our streets, our stores, and our parks, while men just turn and walk away, saying, "I wish someone would do something about that."

Your Creed and your Code should slice through the fog of woke self-righteousness. In Hawaii, there are times when the volcano Kīlauea or Mauna Loa starts blowing out a lot of ash. Sometimes, there is no flow of burning lava—just smoke. The smoke fills the air and at times drifts a couple of hundred miles across the sea, all the way to here on O'ahu. We call it vog. That is what we see so much of today: all smoke and no fire.

It is time to stand for what is right and true. It is time to take action. It is time for your actions to show your beliefs. Opinions don't reveal your convictions. Faith *in action* does. St. James said that, "for as the body apart from the spirit is dead, so also faith apart from works is dead" (James 2:26). He said, "Faith without works is dead" (see James 2:17). Worse than that, not only is it dead: it kills the faith of those who are searching for a reason for hope but only see weak-willed, passive, "nice" Christian man-boys.

Living by the Creed that you wrote down means more than just giving something your intellectual nod of approval. That Creed is at the core of everything you dwell on, reason over, choose, and act on. It not only guides you along your course: it propels you and even compels you. It makes decisions simple. Your course of action may not be easy, but the choice will be clear. My mother's sage advice was this: "When you are having difficulty making a decision, pursue the harder thing. That is usually the right one."

Prudence is considered "charioteer of the virtues." It is the habit of always seeking the true good. This usually makes the choice clear, but we still must decide, act, and pursue the true good with resolute determination.

So, take action. Join your church council, teach catechism, start a men's group, run for the school board or the city council, join the Parent-Teacher Association, start a community watch team in partnership with your local police, pray the Rosary outside a local Planned Parenthood clinic, or support a local shelter for women.

Do something.

You know what it is. Do it.

St. Paul gave no quarter to the weak-willed. When he rebuked a church, he did not say it in that sweet, passive demeanor we project on saints. No, he got right out in the open, as he once wrote, "You stupid Galatians!" (see Gal. 3:1). That wasn't very nice, was it? But it was right to confront them and challenge them to be better. That was the true good. Sometimes it takes a bit of a street fighter to stand up for what is right.

When I tested for my first ninja black belt, I paraphrased King David's Code and made it my own. Each black-belt candidate got to have his motto painted in big letters on the dojo wall during his six-month test. Part of our test required us to scale a sheer, cold, rocky cliff on the south end of Zuma Beach in Malibu. It was basically straight up, and in some places, the only thing you could use as a grip was a quarter-inch (or less) crease in the cliff. My Creed on the wall, based on Psalm 61, read: "Lead me to the rock too high to climb, and I will climb it."

As we cling to that rappelling rope, scaling a steep cliff, we can shout out to God for help, for He says: "Not by might, not by power, but by my Spirit" (Zech. 4:6).

David asked God to lead him to do the hard thing—in fact, the impossible thing. Don't you want God to ask the same of you? He has a habit of doing this. You remember Goliath, right? Being in God's will and doing the hard thing is the only place to be. When we follow God's will, it seems that we have run out of options. We have only one place to look to for strength and help. And when we are at the end of our resources, our ideas, our gifts, and our strength, then we get to see God do stuff. We get to see Him charging in like the cavalry.

Why walk a trail that leads you far from God? Why not walk a little over there, on the wild side, on the road less traveled? That is where God is. That is where He is doing stuff. He is always up to something, and when you are there on that path, you get to do stuff with Him. You get to see Him in action. The Holy Spirit gives us superhero powers, you know.

Just pray a dangerous prayer: "Lord, send me." If you try that one out, you'd better hang on to your horses and get ready for the ride of your life. God will use you in surprising and adventurous ways.

In the film *Open Range*, when a ranch is threatened by a despotic neighboring rancher, a ranch hand asks his boss, "You reckon those cows are worth getting killed over?" The boss's response: "The cows are one thing. But one man telling another man where he can go in this country is another."

Will you allow the cancel culture to bully you into submission? Or will you make a stand for your family and friends? The woke are just bullies who wear the armor of self-righteousness.

Are you ready to make a stand? Cowards are unreliable and that makes them dangerous. But real men have the courage and integrity to do the right thing every time. Which one are you?

In the days when cowboys first went out west, just making a go of it in day-to-day life out on the open range required a certain heroism. And so it does today. Pray a dangerous prayer: "Lord, send me into the fray of the everyday, and by Your power and love, I will make a stand for Your will." God is going to dig on that. As my friend Jason Jones and his sons pray each day: "Lord, place us between evil and the vulnerable."

What does it mean to be truly dangerous? Does it not first mean to be ready to do a certain violence to the appetites and passions that drive us? Then we will have that certitude to stand when the world takes the fight to us.

True nobility, true humility, is power under control. Do not confuse weakness with meekness. Meekness is the strength and courage to yield ourselves actively to God's will. It takes power to be able to do that. Weakness is the opposite of meekness. The best war horses are meek, not weak. They exude great power and bravery in the face of battle, but they do that as they yield completely to the will of the cowboy riding them. Meekness is power—power under control.

That is the kind of dangerous man that God is calling you to be: a man with his strength and courage yielded actively to God in the midst of battle. God can do great good through a man like that.

You are that man. God has chosen you. Will you step up? Are you willing to be dangerous?

The Spiritual Battle

St. Paul says, "For we do not wrestle against flesh and blood, but against the rulers, against the authorities, against the cosmic powers over this present darkness, against the spiritual forces of evil in the heavenly places" (Eph. 6:12). Men must come to grips with the fact that we were born into the midst of the crossfire of a spiritual battlefield. The battle rages all around us, and yet so many men don't even realize that they are in a fight to the death.

St. Michael and his angels have been waging this battle with the evil one and his minions for centuries. Now it is your turn to enter into the fray—whether you like it or not.

Jesus said to Peter, "I tell you, you are Peter, and on this rock I will build my church, and the gates of hell will not prevail against it" (Matt. 16:18). Think about that. Gates don't attack people. We are to attack the gates. Your weapons are prayer, the virtues, and the sacraments. We wield the power of the Holy Spirit and the name of Jesus as we storm the gates of Hell. "The weapons of our warfare are not of the flesh but have divine power to destroy strongholds" (2 Cor 10:4).

Do you see? We are not meant to be in a defensive posture. We are meant to be on the attack. Look at this passage in Ephesians about the armor of God: there is no armor protecting the back. We are not to run from battle but stand firm and press on.

> Finally, be strong in the Lord and in the strength of his might. Put on the whole armor of God, that you may be able to stand against the schemes of the devil. For we do not wrestle against flesh and blood, but against the rulers, against the authorities, against the cosmic powers over this present darkness, against the spiritual forces of evil in the heavenly places. Therefore take up the whole armor of God, that you may be able to withstand in the evil day, and having done all, to stand firm. Stand therefore, having fastened on the belt of truth, and having put on the breastplate of righteousness, and, as shoes for your feet, having put on the readiness given by the gospel of peace. In all circumstances take up the shield of faith, with which you can extinguish all the flaming darts of the evil one; and take the helmet of salvation, and the sword of the Spirit, which is the word of God. (Eph. 6:10–17)

If there is nothing protecting our backs, then we are not to be on the defensive. We are to take the fight to the enemy. Jesus even said, "I have not come to bring peace, but a sword" (Matt. 10:34). There is a peace that passes understanding which is most certainly the presence of the Holy Spirit, but there is also a peace that comes after winning a war. We must win that peace by the grace of God.

In his *History of Christendom*, Warren Carroll mentions a Spanish general who had innumerable scars—but only on the front of him. He never once turned his back and fled from the enemy.

As you press on as a man and as the spiritual head of your home, be assured that "no weapon that is fashioned against you shall succeed" (Isa. 54:17). Learn to fight spiritual combat. Pray a blessing over your home with holy water, making the Sign of the Cross on every doorway. Bless your wife and your children in the same way. Bless your entire yard, and all of its entrances. Keep a crucifix over each entrance to your home. Be the man and stand guard. "Be strong and courageous. Do not be frightened, and do not be dismayed, for the LORD your God is with you wherever you go" (Josh. 1:9). "God gave us a spirit not of fear but of power and love and self-control" (2 Tim. 1:7).

Satan is a coward. He sneaks around the back door to see whom he can attack unawares. Jesus flicks him away like a gnat. As He said, "By the finger of God, I cast out Satan" (see Luke 11:20).

People sometimes ask me if I come under spiritual attack while we are on the road filming *Long Ride Home*. I tell them no. We don't come under attack: we are *on* the attack. Sometimes we face demonic resistance, but we are the ones on the attack. They are on the run. "Resist the devil and he will flee" (James 4:7).

The Physical Fight

Though a Louis L'Amour cowboy is slow to anger, he can only be pushed so far. Don't cuss in front of women or children. Don't doubt his word; don't cross his boundary unless you are invited; don't mess with someone in vulnerable circumstances. A cowboy knows how to settle things with words, but if it comes down to it, he knows how to fight. When push comes to shove, he is no pushover.

Cowboys are ready and able to fight, but they are also good at diffusing touchy situations. They are not the ones to throw the first punch or to slap iron before another man goes for his gun, yet they can think and act with coolness all the while.

The fastest way to make them angry, though, is to call them a liar, a thief, or a cheater. They can take a punch and get knocked down, but they will keep getting up until they either win the fight or are beaten. They don't have any quit in them. When a cowboy loses, it does not mean that he is a loser; it means that he will keep on learning and getting stronger until he wins.

As a young boy, I had started school a year sooner than I was supposed to, so I was always the youngest and the smallest in my class. We also moved a lot, so I was always the new kid in school. I was tested a lot by bullies all the way until I got into high school. I lost every fight.

As a young man and a father myself, I remember mowing the grass in the backyard one afternoon, and it was as if the Holy Spirit tapped me on the shoulder. He had something to say to me. "Does the fact that you lost every fight when you were young make you a loser? No," he went on to say. "Even though you knew you were probably going to lose to the bigger, older bully, you did not back down. You fought. That doesn't make you a loser. It makes you a fighter."

I shared that because I know some of you right now are facing that same kind of challenge in your lives. I am proud of you for not backing down, and so is God.

God made men big in their bones and strong in their muscles and sinews for a reason. Men, by their nature, are meant to be protectors. God infused men with this warrior-hero nature that we must develop before the day of real testing comes.

Long Ride Home cast member Kainoa Li is a master of Lua. He has been training in this Hawaiian martial art his whole life. He told me that when he was in high school, an older, bigger boy kept bullying him. Finally, it was time for the showdown. To a trained martial artist, a street fighter's punch looks as if it is coming at you in slow motion. When the other kid threw a punch, Kai smoothly reacted by doing as Jesus instructed: he turned his cheek so that the punch just grazed him. He then said to the other boy, "I hope you feel better now." Then he turned and walked away. Had another punch been thrown, though, it would have been the bully's last.

Every man should be trained in how to fight and how to wield a weapon. He also needs to be fit enough to do so, and he needs to be willing and able to do unthinkable things, to the degree required, to stop an assailant in order to protect himself and his loved ones. When you become a trained martial artist, you can inflict a lot of pain without necessarily inflicting a lot of damage—though you *can* inflict a lot of damage when necessary. If there are multiple attackers, the defender has no choice but to use maximum force on the first ones to attack him. They will need to be dealt with in a devastating way so they are no longer in the fight.

If you are not trained in basic fighting skills, you need to train and learn. Jab, punch, hook, uppercut, front snap kick, sidekick, and a back kick are great skills to have, along with basic blocking abilities and the fitness to outlast your opponent. It's also helpful to learn how to safely and effectively handle a gun and be willing to use it, if needed.

A great benefit of developing your fighting skills is that the untrained have no choice but to use ultimate force, whereas a trained martial artist can make surgical strikes to disarm and disable. An aggressor knows his intentions and how far he is willing to go. You must therefore assume the worst in the aggressor and respond with all necessary force.

There is also this talk that you need to have with yourself. You need to think things over and determine just how far you are willing to go in a fight. You need to ponder what it would be like to hit someone in the throat with an extended knuckle fist or to push your fingers two inches deep into an assailant's eye sockets. You need to think about it, feel it, make a decision once and for all, and then tuck it away in the back of your mind for the day when you may need it. You need to decide what circumstances it would take for you to go berserk—to go Viking on someone.

I see so many men these days with arms that look like they are just dangling from their shoulders by the ligaments, with no muscle, and they look as if they do not do cardio training. They will be out of breath and out of the fight in only a couple of minutes. Every man has a duty to those he loves to be fit enough to outlast his opponent.

Trust me: if you're calling the police, it's already too late. They usually can't get there in time to help. In spite of their best efforts, they usually get there in time to ask, "What just happened?" These days, we don't handcuff offenders: we handcuff our police. We let criminals right back out on the street with no bail and no penalties. You need to be prepared to defend your family, and they need to be prepared to defend themselves as well.

I got to test two of my sons for their black belts. My other son and my daughter made it halfway to black belt. This was something that I required of them. My daughter has told me how there has been occasion to be thankful for that training.

I have earned teaching degrees in several different martial arts as well as black belts in the ninja combative way. Trained martial artists are, first and foremost, spatially aware. They are tuned in to the attitudes and intentions of the people around them. They seem to exude a confident awareness that puts an aggressor looking for easy prey on notice that they are not likely to be an easy target or a passive victim.

I am not saying here that martial artists look like macho tough guys whose mommies never loved them. No, they look confident, alert, and fit. They are, for the most part, easy to get along with. They know they are good fighters and they have nothing to prove to anyone else. They would rather walk away, if possible, but they are ready and willing to respond when provoked. Most people may not even take note of their demeanor, but a bully can see it and will tend to avoid it.

Martial artists avoid places and people where unnecessary trouble may erupt. The best form of self-defense is not to be there in the first place. I was teaching a women's self-defense class once, and one of them asked, "What if I am at an ATM at night and I sense that someone is coming up behind me? What's a technique that I can use?"

I responded, "That is easy. I can teach you a technique so that you never have to worry about a situation like that ever again." All the attendees' ears perked up. As they gazed attentively, I said, "It's simple. Do not go to an ATM machine at night." A little prudence can go a long way.

Still, when it comes to self-defense, violence may be the only option. If so, we must be prepared to be violent.

One of a man's primary purposes is to be a protector. Perhaps one thing you could do is start or join a community watch group. Train your family in awareness skills. Teach them some fighting skills. Have them all carry an easy-access alarm that sets off a screeching siren by just pressing a small canister that can be attached to the outside of a backpack.

The dangerous man is spatially aware. My wife, Cindy, for example, knows just where I want to sit in a restaurant so that I can always see what is going on. Recently, I joined EWTN TV host Doug Barry, who is a trained fighter and man of God, in a little café for breakfast. When we both went for the same chair at the same table, we realized that we were both automatically going for the alpha chair. He grinned and said, "Spatial awareness, right?" In that situation, we both knew that we each had each other's back. So, regardless of who sat where, we were both scanning the room for danger. This is not some schizoid behavior. It's not a nervous or neurotic habit. It's just second nature to us. It brings peace, not anxiety.

As Cindy and I walk along certain streets, she turns to gaze at me, as I do to her. We are actually taking turns scanning what is behind us. If there is a creeper nearing us, she just casually glides to the other side of me. We don't walk close to bushes or vans. Because we are vigilant, we are at ease.

There is no man more dangerous than a man who stands by his personal Creed and his Code. He fights to retain his honor, knowing that a man's honor is earned only with struggle and testing, and that it can be lost in a heartbeat.

A man like that knows when he is right. There is no quit in him. Be Dangerous.

The weak can be terrible when they wish
to appear strong, and he was such a man,
darkly vengeful and unforgetting.

—Louis L'Amour, *The Walking Drum*

Rule 5

Bridle Your Passion: Let Good Things Run Wild

Victory is won not in miles but in inches.
Win a little now, hold your ground,
and later, win a little more.

—Louis L'Amour, *The Walking Drum*

Out west, a man's horse was sometimes the closest thing he had to a friend. He took care of that horse. He made sure that it was well shod so it could handle tough terrain. He saw to it that the horse was fed properly and often—but not too often. To steal a man's horse was a hanging offense because it most likely meant leaving him with no way to make a living—or, worse yet, leaving him for dead.

My dad had in his office a big painting that my mom had given him. It reminded her of him. It was of a herd of wild mustangs running before the driving wind of a coming thunderstorm. They were wild and free. Their hooves thundered and kicked up dust. Every sinew exuded strength.

The harshness and danger of a mustang's environment requires him to be fully alive and alert, with his ears twitching at every sound, wary of the danger of mountain lions, wolves, and even bears. The terrain itself is dangerous; even a small injury can lead to an agonizing and untimely death.

Think of your passions, your appetites, and your desires as a powerful horse that you—the rider—must guide, rein in, and then, at the right time, release in its full, resplendent power.

What does it take for your passions to turn into upward desires to be strong, to be nourished, to be tested and true—and yet not subject to the dangers and pitfalls of the untamed?

The Bible says, "I will give you a new heart [I will give you new and right desires], and a new spirit I will put within you. And I will remove the heart of stone from your flesh and give you a heart of flesh" (Ezek. 36:26).

I do not want to be driven by passion; I want to be led by my upward desire for God. The Latin root for *passion* means "to suffer." But desire is very different. Its root word means "to have a longing for the stars." It means to look up for your purpose and meaning and to be led by them, as opposed to being driven by passion and appetites.

If there was ever an image of a man's properly ordered passions and desires, it would be this description in the book of Job:

> Do you give the horse his might? Do you clothe his neck with a mane? Do you make him leap like the locust? His majestic snorting is terrifying. He paws in the valley and exults in his strength; he goes out to meet the weapons. He laughs at fear and is not dismayed; he does not turn back from the sword. (Job 39:19-22)

A wild mustang has never experienced what is to be saddled and bridled and ridden. When a wild mustang is first captured, it is brought into a circular corral, and the cowboy begins to walk him. By the way the cowboy steps in and points, or twirls a rope, or speaks to the horse, he can begin to redirect the horse in the opposite direction. In time, the horse begins to feel that *telos*, that purpose to be joined to a rider. It begins to twist its ears so that they are always facing toward its new master. It becomes more and more attentive to the cowboy and comes to long for that connection. It learns—and by its nature, it wants—to be more and more responsive.

Then comes the time when the bridle is put on the horse. Next, the saddle is placed on it but not cinched. As the horse becomes comfortable, the man will step into the stirrup for just a few moments. Soon, he'll lean over the saddle and lie across it. Finally comes that great moment when the man brings himself all the way up onto the saddle and sits astride the horse. The horse has already been taught how to be led by the bridle, so the horse and the man ride for a while. Before long, they become one, as the horse finds its telos—its purpose—in serving the man.

The horse becomes fully alive as it has learned to submit actively to the cowboy. In so doing, both enter into a partnership and an adventure that neither could ever experience in the wild. The horse begins to long for the touch of the cowboy. It wants to be ridden. In fact, as the cowboy begins to saddle him up, he begins to lick his lips in anticipation, tasting the endorphins that its excitement has released in its mouth.

I read a news story just the other day about a ranch horse in Wyoming. The rancher had chosen this horse from among all of the ranch horses because of its spirit. The horse could outwork even him! From time to time, when the wild mustangs would roam by, his horse would gallop out and whinny to them. It would run with them for a little while and then return. But one day, it galloped off and never came back.

For years, the man spent every weekend, sometimes with the help of his dad, out riding and looking for that horse. He put out a notice to the Bureau of Land Management to keep an eye out for the horse; he would be easy to spot because he was at least a couple hands taller than the wild mustangs. Years went by, but the man and his father never did find the horse. Two months before this article came out, the rancher's father passed away, and yet the man still rode out in search of the horse, missing the companionship of both his horse and his dad.

Then, a couple of weeks ago, a miracle happened. Perhaps the man's dad was praying in Heaven. The Bureau had spotted the horse and corralled him. The rancher hitched up his horse trailer, jumped into his truck, and rode, hell-bent for leather to see his horse. He wondered, *Would the horse even recognize him? Would it be too wild to ride?* As he jumped out of his truck and sauntered over to the corral, his horse spotted him, whinnied, and loped over to him. The horse had lost well over four hundred pounds but otherwise seemed to be healthy.

The man and the horse said their hellos; the horse nudged him with his nose, for he longed for the cowboy's touch. The man bridled the horse, threw a saddle on it, and they rode together once again. It was as if the horse had never forgotten him, or the bridle, or how to step up into a trailer. Today, the horse is gaining weight every day and the rancher once again rides him as his favorite workhorse.

Maybe this is your story. Once upon a time, you reigned in and directed your appetites, your passions. But then they began to run loose. Now, like that horse, you're broken down. Your soul is gaunt.

It is time for you to mount up again and say to your horse— your appetites, passions, and desires—"I am the rider. I am your master. I will guide you; I will set you on a course of true free-dom, and you will be a powerful working horse again. Your power, which drives you like a thunderstorm into the wild, will become a longing to serve our highest calling. You will serve me as I serve God."

This is your job. This is self-mastery. You are the rider and the horse. Your job is to break and bridle your passions so you can become strong, so you can achieve your telos, so you can become whole. Turn the drivenness of your own passion from your will to God's will. Let your heart soar with the upward yearning for God and the adventure that He has for you.

God made the horse for man. A horse's greatest dignity, the essence of his telos, is to be in relationship with and to be submissive to his rider. He is never freer and happier than when he is responsive to his rider. This will be true of you and your passions too.

The heroes in Louis L'Amour's books are not given to drunk-enness or excessive gambling. When someone provokes a fight with them in a bar, they are the ones who are not too drunk to win. They always have their wits about them — an advantage that will decide the outcome of nearly any fight.

What does it take for a man living in mediocrity to change his trajectory and to arrive at the greatness that God has in-tended for him, and for him to experience and live in the ful-fillment of all that he desires, all that God has placed in his heart? Think about it. Does it not begin with self-mastery — with temperance? Does it not take a circumspect and powerful au-tonomy that owns up to our decisions and actions? Does it not take a sense of purpose and a pursuit of our own telos, which in turn propels us on to that unique high calling that God has for each one of us?

So, before we move on, before we begin our quest, we must get real. We must get gritty and get tough-minded and begin right now with the mastery of our passions and *ourselves*.

When I was in elementary school, I read a book about the famous racehorse Man o' War. Until I read that book, I always thought the goal of the rider on a racehorse was just to make that horse run as fast as he could. But I learned that the rider had to know when to hold him back, when to let him run, and when to urge him on to his top speed. That is our place in mastering our appetites and passions, guiding them with our upward desire for God's will and His order.

So it is with our passions and the natural desires that we have for our fellow created things. There is a time and place, a natural order, in which they are to be experienced and enjoyed. For example, there is a time to enjoy a whiskey and a cigar on the deck as you read in solitude or while you enjoy the company of other men. But to be constantly siphoning the whiskey from your desk drawer at the office or while driving a semitruck is disordered.

Sexual intimacy properly ordered and reserved for the nuptial union of a marriage between a man and a woman can be—let's face it—awesome, for there it becomes not just a physical union but also a certain cleaving of the souls. Because the soul joins in a unique way to the other during sex, someone who chooses to have multiple sexual partners fractures his own soul until it becomes just like the Scarecrow in *The Wizard of Oz*. "Part of me is over here and part of me is over there." Outside of the order and blessing that God intended in marriage, sex can be so destructive.

Men, you are under full-on attack by the demon pornography. You must have a strategy to defeat that enemy.

When I was young, you had to go out of your way to see pornography. Now that enemy is not just knocking on the door: he's breaking it down.

Every time someone turns on the TV or the computer or picks up a smartphone, the seduction of the enemy—the seduction that weakens men and uses women—is right there. Men, we must win that battle.

St. John Paul II wrote that the problem with pornography is not that it shows too much of a woman but that it shows too little. In other words, the focus is only on her body but not on the beauty of her soul. It makes the person an object of lust instead of the subject of love. You must learn to bridle, restrain, and guide this passion into God's plan and, in so doing, experience the true pleasure and blessing that it is intended to be.

The drive and passion for career success and financial gain is another area that wants to buck us off. Desiring success in our careers is noble and worthy, but we can end up being driven by ambition and the lust for money, power, and prestige. The workaholic robs his family of his attention and time that they deserve—and need. If we are productive and provide for our families, we are living in accordance with God's high calling for us. This includes our desire to help our team and our company to reach their goals, as opposed to remaining fixed only on our own selfish ambition. Let our desire be to serve God and neighbor, to provide for our families and for the Church. Scripture says, "Whatever you do, work heartily, as for the Lord and not for men, knowing that from the Lord you will receive the inheritance as your reward" (Col. 3:23–24).

Of course, addictions to drinking and drugs also rob us of our telos. God implanted in our hearts a desire to get "high," to find a happiness beyond anything we can imagine. But that longing can be satisfied only by *Him*. He is the fulfillment of all desire. Disordered passion is simply an unbridled, excessive craving for created goods in a way that is not good.

So the more we drink or dope, the emptier we feel inside. An early Church Father wrote that it is like someone eating air; he succeeds in filling himself only with more emptiness. That great cosmic chasm in our hearts is actually an infinite emptiness, an infinite tabernacle with an infinite capacity, for it is placed there by God for God to make it His dwelling place. The emptiness we experience will remain there until we invite Jesus, our infinite God, to make His home in us. For are we not the temples of the Holy Spirit? If we are designed with the capacity to be God's vessels, how great must that emptiness be unless and until we say yes to Jesus, who is knocking on the door of our hearts? As powerful as our Creator and the Creator of the universe is, He has given us the power to say yes or no to Him.

Perhaps you have said yes to Him and invited Him in, but there are still certain areas in which you have not quite opened the door to Him yet. Perhaps it is an area of passion that you are clinging to instead of clinging to Him. Why not stop here and pray and give all of yourself to Jesus?

My dad use to tell the story of how hunters in Africa would hunt for monkeys to sell to zoos. They would place a piece of fruit in a gourd that was tied to a stake. The monkey would come by and reach into the gourd to grab the fruit. With the fruit in his fist, the opening of the gourd was too small for the monkey to pull his fist out. He would stay there, frustrated, trying again and again to get his hand out of the gourd without letting go of the forbidden fruit. Then, finally, the hunter would come by and club him on the head.

Is this not what the enemy does when he tempts our passion? We hang on and hang on to something that we can never really have or that will never really satisfy us until finally we are imprisoned.

The passion of anger can be a good thing too. Scripture says, "Be angry and do not sin" (Eph. 4:26). God gave us anger so that we could recognize injustice and then turn that into the determination to do something about it. But disordered anger not only kills relationships: it kills the out-of-control man. Disordered anger destroys.

Most of our anger comes from the failure of life or others to live up to our expectations. We must either adjust our expectations or develop a plan to change things for the good. Out-of-control anger makes everything all about *us*. Men who do not seek out the source of their anger, who don't grapple with it or do something positive with it, eventually explode, hurting not only themselves but everyone around them.

Just like a mighty racehorse, our passions run best and fulfill their purpose, and so fulfill *us*, when they are bridled, reined in, and released, guided and directed by a man whose soul's primary desire is to delight in the will and the presence of God. In that way, our passions reach their ultimate goodness, and we let good things run wild.

The book of Revelation is full of images of horses and riders. There are two I find striking:

> I saw heaven opened, and behold, a white horse! The one sitting on it is called Faithful and True, and in righteousness he judges and makes war. (19:11)

> The armies of heaven, arrayed in fine linen, white and pure, were following him on white horses. (19:14)

These two images depict the perfect power and purity of soul of a person who is totally yielded to God. There is first the example of Christ and then of us, His army. Let this be the image of our passions and appetites, properly purified, properly ordered, and transformed to an upward desire for God and His will.

The key to being free from pornography, lasciviousness, sexual promiscuity, alcoholism, drug addiction, anger, greed, and pride is to train our hearts and minds to love God back, and that is done in meditation on His Word, in prayer, in Eucharistic adoration, in the sacraments, and through works of mercy.

The psalm says that, with God's power, "my arms can bend a bow of bronze" (18:34). A bow is at full potential when the arrow is notched and the string pulled back. Then it's ready to be released—for good purpose or bad. So is the potential of our either yielding to passion or releasing our desires and letting that arrow take flight in God's purpose. This battle is won in prayer. It is said of the monks of the desert in the first centuries of the Church that, throughout the day, their prayers were sent up to God as arrows. So let your arrows of praise, of love, of intercession fly up to the heart of God. This is what will set you free from being controlled by your passions. When we find the mark that God has set for us and release the arrow when He gives the word, good things happen.

You see, the word for *sin* in both the New Testament and the Old is an archer's term meaning "to miss the mark." An archer takes a deep breath and then focuses on the target. If he gets distracted and loses focus, he will miss the mark. And so it is that the key to defeating sins driven by your appetites and passions is to focus all your attention on God.

The key is prayer, adoration before the Eucharist, and meditating on God's Word. In the Song of Solomon, the king (who, by the way, represents Jesus) says to the woman (who represents a soul in love with Jesus), "Your eyes are like doves" (Song of Sol.

4:1). It turns out that a turtledove's eyes are unique in that they can focus on only one thing at a time. Even as an archer brings his whole attention to focus on the target, so the soul who wants to be free from the bondage of passion and wants to soar toward the heart of God must let God be its sole focus.

When you develop that personal relationship with God by spending time with Him every day, you will not want to risk losing that intimacy with God for some fleeting pleasure. The thought of offending God will be detestable to you.

Do you want to bridle your passions? Spend time with God. Run to Him in prayer when you are tempted. Have strategies for breaking the devil's hold on your mind—such as pulling out your rosary, getting up and going for a walk, or listening to an audio version of a sacred book. Take action. Defeat the enemy. Your prayers put an arrow in the enemy's heart. "Resist the devil and he will flee" (James 4:7).

I remember a long time ago, down at County Line Beach near Malibu, watching three inebriated young guys drag a canoe down the roadside cliff to the beach. This was not an outrigger canoe; it was not meant to be paddled on the ocean. I overheard one of them yelling out orders and realized that they intended to load a big ice chest full of beer in the canoe and then all crawl in and paddle it about ten miles down along the coast. It was so comical, and I laughed so hard at their antics that my eyes watered and my contact lenses fell out.

As they began to try to paddle through the shore break, one of the guys fell overboard, while the two others continued to paddle, battling to get outside the breakers. To my amazement, in a lull between big waves, they made it out while the leader of the pack continued to bark out orders as if he were Captain Bligh. Things were looking bleak as they began to drift toward a hazardous reef to the south called Bomburas. The remaining crew member freaked out, and he bailed out of the ship as the captain yelled, "Mutiny!"

I began to realize that his situation was quickly coming to a disaster as he was being swept nearer to the shallow outer reef. So I ran down the beach, grabbed my board, and paddled out to rescue him from his own foolishness. As I neared him, I slowed down and became quite cautious. By this time, he had fallen out of the canoe along with the beer chest and desperately clung to both the ice chest and the canoe. Any victim can be quite dangerous to the rescuer, so a certain cautious strategy must be used, but Captain Bligh was out of control.

He was gradually floating into the reef, as the leathery seaweed started to snarl up and entangle him. As I got within five feet, I ordered him to let go of the canoe and the beer so I could grab him and bring him onto my surfboard. But he would not. He clung to them both for dear life. I realized my only hope of saving him was to grab the rope tied to the front of the canoe and paddle and pull him, the canoe, and the beer back to the beach.

As I paddled him toward the beach, he continually screamed out, "Mutiny!" It was more than just hysterically funny; it was pitiful. This man almost squandered his life and the lives of his friends by clinging to something that would never save him, as so many do today.

That is the state of a man who seeks consolation in anything other than God. We need to let go and trust God. Let Him be our aim and our consolation.

It was our great philosophers Socrates, Plato, and Aristotle who taught us to pursue happiness and revealed that the source of true happiness is the pursuit of the virtues of self-mastery (temperance), prudence, justice, and fortitude. Aristotle said that virtue is "that which makes both a person and what he does good."

The Book of Wisdom—which, by the way, was removed from Protestant Bibles—affirms these four virtues: "For [Wisdom] teaches temperance and prudence, justice and fortitude, and nothing in life is more useful for men than these" (see 8:7).

These virtues are also referred to as the moral virtues or the cardinal virtues. The word *cardinal* comes from the Latin word meaning "hinge," like the hinge on a gate, for truly the virtues are the doorway to happiness. It also refers to the four points of the ancient navigator's compass. The virtues point the way to our telos. There can be no surer guide than these virtues for a man in pursuit of happiness. All men, even atheists, can and should aspire to them, but Christians infused with God's grace are more readily able to do so.[4] For the Holy Spirit infuses us with the theological virtues of faith, hope, and love, and these, in turn, empower the four cardinal virtues.

All virtues are, in fact, wrapped up in the virtue of love. It is through the Holy Spirit's infusion of these powerful graces that we are able to live lives of virtue.

In the realm of temperance, or self-mastery, Aristotle's teaching is simple: "All things in moderation." He was pointing out that overindulging even in good things can make those things bad for us.

I would say, though, as a good Catholic, that even our commitment to moderation must at times be moderated. Catholics fast, but we also feast. Perhaps there is a time, a rare time, and a place to have a little bit too much of a manly beverage or to

---

[4] For more on the virtues, see my book *Deep Adventure: The Way of Heroic Virtue.*

indulge in more than one piece of pie. St. Thomas Aquinas lays it out in no uncertain terms by defining an effeminate man as one who indulges himself in pleasure. This is not to say that we can't enjoy the good things in life. But we must enjoy them according to God's order.

As we rein in and guide our passions, we are telling them who is boss. "I will direct you," we say. "You are not going to take off like a stubborn horse and carry me with you or try to buck me off as you make a dead run for the consolation of the alfalfa back at the barn. I am the rider; you are the horse." Remember, St. Francis called his body "Brother Ass."

But it is the virtue of self-mastery that holds the reins on our passions and directs them in pursuit of the other virtues. G. K. Chesterton wrote that the four cardinal virtues are ones of restraint, but when it comes to the three theological virtues, which are based on a personal relationship with God, we can let the reins out and let that horse run wild. Because He is an infinite God, we can never love Him too much or hope too much or have too much faith. As we surfers say, we can "go for it!"

Chesterton also said that the good news about walls of orthodoxy is that it lets good things run wild.

You see, natural goods such as sex, food, and drink are temporal things. So we must enjoy them in a limited way. But because God is love, we can let our desire for Him run wild. We can love Him back enthusiastically. The root of the word *enthusiasm* is *en theos*, meaning "in God." For Jesus commanded us, "You shall love the Lord your God with all your heart, and with all your soul, and with all your mind" (Matt. 22:37). The only desire that can be allowed to run wild and totally free is our upward yearning for God. So let your love for God run as wild as a mustang bounding up a mountain to a fresh stream.

Once you start building this relationship, you won't be able to stand the thought of losing the joy and the consolation you receive from spending time with God in prayer and from meditating on the Bible.

By the way, did you know that the word *meditate* in Hebrew is really a cowboy word? It means "ruminate," which is what a cow does in chewing grass, swallowing it, and then burping it up, chewing it some more, and swallowing it again several times. Read God's Word in the morning, and throughout the day, chew on it like a piece of beef jerky. Indulge yourself in the fine wine of God's love letter to you, the Bible. You know that the shame of sin leaves you hiding from God, as Adam and Eve did; let the thought of losing that intimacy with God be your sin repellent.

I remember sitting outside that cabin I built in Montana. As the sun set behind me and its golden glow lit up the Glacier Peaks in front of me, I began to get little bites from bugs that I could not even see. The next time I drove into the little two-building town of Polebridge for supplies, I asked the clerks about those bugs. They said, "Oh, we call those little bugs 'no-see-ums.' If you smoke a cigar while you are out at sunset, the smoke will keep them away."

Up to that point in my life—and I was in my late forties—I had never smoked anything, but I was determined to enjoy my sunsets. So I bought the only cigars they had: Swisher Sweets. And you know what, the smoke of those cigars did the trick. I soon graduated to finer cigars, my favorite being the Arturo Fuente 8-5-8, and then I even developed my own line of seven blends of cigars called "The Seven Virtues Cigars." The milder blends are named after the four cardinal virtues and the Maduros are named after the three theological virtues.

That is how you defeat the demonic "no-see-ums" that tempt you. Offering up the smoke of your prayers and praise to God drives them away. As Revelation says, "The smoke of the incense rose with the prayers of the saints from the hand of the angel before God" (8:4).

Do you remember the sage advice of the cowboy Curly in the film *City Slickers*? At some point, he stuck up his black-leather-gloved hand and pointed his index finger to the sky and said, "One thing." It left the character Mitch stunned and perplexed. When they asked him what he meant, he just simply responded: "That is for you to figure out."

Jesus answered that question for us when He spoke to the busy, preoccupied, stressed-out drivenness of Martha: "Martha, Martha, you are anxious and troubled about many things; one thing is needful" (Luke 10:41–42). And what was that "one thing"? Jesus pointed to Martha's sister, Mary, who was content just to sit at the Lord's feet, and said, "She has chosen the better part" (see Luke 10:42). When we spend time with God, our desire for Him and His will eclipses our passions. Spend time in prayer with God. He will change your heart.

Fr. Robert Spitzer summarizes these God-implanted upward yearnings that are common to all men as five desires: "justice, truth, beauty, love and a desire to go home."[5]

We have a fallen nature, a heart tainted by an inclination to sin. This concupiscence can be healed only by a real relationship with God and by the power of His grace. White-knuckling alone to try to overcome our concupiscence won't do it. Our will alone

---

[5] See "Our Desire for Five Transcendentals Shows That God Exists," Catholic Apologetics Institute of North America, https:// cainaweb.org/five_transcendentals/.

can't do it. In fact, that notion is known as Pelagianism, and it's an ancient heresy. No one can perfect himself and earn his own way to Heaven. We need God's grace. We need God to help us by giving us that new heart with new and right desires.

The *Catechism of the Catholic Church* says that concupiscence has to do with an appetite for something that nature requires, such as food or sexual union. Concupiscence is not sin but it can be the "tinder for sin"; "it cannot harm those who do not consent" (CCC 1264).

In his Letter to the Romans, St. Paul spoke about his own battle:

> I do not understand my own actions. For I do not do what I want, but I do the very thing I hate.... For I do not do the good I want, but the evil I do not want is what I keep on doing.... I delight in the law of God, in my inner being, but I see in my members another law waging war against the law of my mind and making me captive to the law of sin which dwells in my members. Wretched man that I am! Who will deliver me from this body of death?" (7:15–24)

The very fact that you feel the war within you is good news. It means that your new nature is transforming you and pushing away your old, fallen nature. This is done not by brute strength of will but by the infusion of God's grace. It is "not by might, not by power, but by my Spirit, says the LORD" (Zech. 4:6).

St. Paul admonished the Corinthians in their immorality but then went on to give them hope: "Therefore, if any one is in Christ, he is a new creation; the old has passed away, behold, the new has come" (2 Cor. 5:17). That your conscience pricks you when you allow yourself to fall to temptation—this tells you that you have new life within you. Your old nature and your new nature are in a fight to the death. Before you came to Christ, you were good friends with sin and with Satan. Not anymore.

How do you win this battle?

Yesterday, a new surfer asked me what the key to surfing is. I told her two things. "First, there is no substitute for time in the water. If you want to learn to surf, go surf." And so it is with the Lord. If we want to live lives of virtue—if we want to walk in God's ways—we need to spend time with the Lord before the Eucharist and in prayer and meditation on His Word.

The second thing that I told her usually makes people laugh when I first tell them. I told her, "Don't fall." But my bride, Cindy, jumped in and said, "I know it sounds funny, but he means it. Don't fall. Your board wants to surf that wave. It is made for that reason. So when you feel as if you are going to fall, try to stay in balance and resist that urge to just fall off or jump off." This is true in your moral battle too. That new nature in you wants to move in the Spirit. It wants you to have a balanced life. It wants you not to fall. So stand strong, and when the enemy is tempting you, resist him and hang on to Jesus as a cowboy on a bucking horse hangs on to his saddle with one hand and raises his hand high with the other. Tighten up your grip on the saddle horn and raise your arm to the Lord in praise.

Just don't fall.

When Cindy was younger, she used to love to ride her horse on a trail through the woods. But she had to be on the alert. Her horse, Peanut, could get mischievous. He loved to turn and ride her right under a branch to try to push her out of the saddle. The Bible warns us and gives us the solution to our passions. "Be sober-minded; be watchful. Your adversary the devil prowls around like a roaring lion, seeking someone to devour" (1 Pet. 5:8). "[Pray] at all times in the Spirit, with all prayer and supplication. To that end, keep alert with all perseverance" (Eph. 6:18).

As God warned Cain, "Sin is crouching at the door; its desire is for you, but you must master it" (Gen. 4:7). God has given us the grace to sit tall in the saddle, to bridle our obstinate, nipping, kicking, bucking-bronco passions and, instead, be led by our new and right desires, infused by the Holy Spirit.

I have had that experience of falling off a horse. I hate to admit it, but it was while the horse was standing perfectly still. I swung my leg over the horse to get off, and the next thing I knew, I was looking up at the stars spinning in front of me from the bounce my head took. But you have heard the saying "Get back on the horse." This is how you do that in your moral life: If you do fall, go to the Lord and confess your sin, asking for His forgiveness. Then go to a priest and make a good confession. God will always forgive those who truly repent. If the battle is raging, you may benefit from going to Confession every week, in order to eradicate a pattern of sin. Sometimes it helps to take our souls out to the woodshed, as the saying goes, and give ourselves a good what for — to make a clean start.

John the Baptist warns us, "Even now the axe is laid to the root of the trees. Every tree therefore that does not bear good fruit is cut down and thrown into the fire" (Matt. 3:10). But the power of the Spirit gives us "both to will and to work for his good pleasure" (Phil. 2:13). The Holy Spirit brings conviction of your sin, to chop that sin out at the root and to restore you to freedom.

Do not mistake the conviction of the Holy Spirit for condemnation. After a criminal is convicted, there follows the penalty phase when the punishment is determined — when the convicted person is condemned to his own unique punishment. But Jesus has already paid the penalty for your sin on the Cross so that, once you repent and confess your sins, you can be free.

> "There is therefore now no condemnation for those who are in Christ Jesus. For the law of the Spirit of life has set you free in Christ Jesus from the law of sin and death.... For all who are led by the Spirit of God are sons of God. For you did not receive the spirit of slavery to fall back into fear, but you have received the Spirit of adoption as sons, by whom we cry, "Abba! Father!" (Rom. 8:1-2, 14-15)

"For freedom Christ has set us free; stand firm therefore, and do not submit again to a yoke of slavery" (Gal. 5:1).

So if you keep falling off that horse, first of all keep trying not to fall. Then look to God for mercy and strength and get back on. "Let us fall into the hands of God and not into the hands of men," as the book of Sirach puts it. "For as great as his majesty is so, too, is his mercy" (see 2:18).

This becomes a no-win situation for Satan. Every time the devil tempts you, you run to God, and if you do fall, you return to God and cling to Him even closer. Satan can't win. "My enemies dug a pit in my way, / but they have fallen into it themselves" (Ps. 57:6).

As I have said before, the best self-defense lesson you can learn is this: "Don't be there." This is true in a spiritual and moral battle too. Avoid dicey situations. As we pray in the confessional, "avoid the near occasion of sin." Adam and Eve should have avoided that tree that God warned them about. Instead, we see Eve lingering there. Adam, who should have been protecting her, is nowhere to be found. When she hung out there long enough, a snake showed up. As a young man hiking the hills of California, I learned to stay on the trail and not wander off into the brush. That's rattlesnake country. I learned to avoid that near occasion.

When a horse senses that there is a snake in the grass, it gets jumpy. It bucks a bit and makes a run for safety. So should we. We need to avoid snakes in the grass—that is, people and places in which sin is lurking to stir up our passions and temptations.

The grace of absolution that you receive in Confession not only brings forgiveness but it also fortifies you with new strength and determination to overcome your sins. And when you go to Confession, you reconcile yourself not only with God and with the whole Body of Christ, but in a very deep and significant way, you are reconciled even with yourself. The shattered turmoil and upside-down divisiveness in your soul gives way to an integrated "oneness of heart."

The battle begins the moment you wake. Go to the Lord in prayer, for "His mercies ... are new every morning" (Lam. 3:22–23). Spend that twenty minutes in the morning praying and meditating on His Word. Bring your heart to the Lord and gaze back at the One who gazes at you and then move on in your day, walking in stride with God. Let Him set the direction and the pace. Always check in with Him.

Fight the good fight and trust in the Lord. Do your part and trust God to do His. "The horse is made ready for the day of battle," says the Book of Proverbs, "but the victory belongs to the LORD" (21:31).

You are ready. The victory is yours.

"There was a Texas Ranger one time who said
that there's no stopping a man who knows
he's in the right and keeps a-coming."

—Louis L'Amour, *Sackett*

Rule 6

Don't Be a Drifter: Seek God's Purpose for You

I watched those in the room with me and was lonely
within myself, for there was in me a great reaching
outwards, a desire to be and to become.

—Louis L'Amour, *Bendigo Shafter*

The most dangerous man who ever lived prayed dangerous prayers. He prayed one night in a grove of ancient, gnarled, thick-trunked trees near an olive press—just across the valley from the place where He would be put to death and would claim His, and our, ultimate victory. As the olive press releases the oil, so, too, the crushing anguish of His soul pressed out drops of blood from His pores.

He is called the Messiah, which means "the anointed one." It means literally "to pour oil out." And so it was that He began that great pouring out of love and redemption when He prayed the most dangerous prayer of all that night at the olive press: "Father, not my will, but Thy will be done."

There it is. Do you see it? There is that most dangerous prayer of all: "Thy will be done."

Are you all in? A cowboy can't just kinda-sorta ride a rodeo bull.

It's time to lay your cards on the table, as cowboys do. Push all your chips into the middle of the table and say, "I'm all in." Because if you are, if you say yes to the vision and plan that God has for you, then demons will tremble when you say His name and mountains will move as you are moved by God's will. It will cost you everything, but it will open vistas of hope and joy you cannot imagine—for you and for those whom your life impacts.

Are you ready to ride for the brand, or are you going to run?

"For I know the plans I have for you, declares the LORD, plans for welfare and not for evil, to give you a future and a hope" (Jer. 29:11). But then He reminds us of the response that He leaves up to us: "You will seek me and find me, when you seek me with all your heart" (Jer. 29:13). He does not say, "If you kinda-sorta seek me." No, He says, "You will find me when you seek me with all your heart." He promises us, "I am the rewarder of those who diligently seek me" (see Heb. 11:6).

To paraphrase Pascal: God hides Himself just enough so that those who really do not want to find Him won't, but those who really want to find Him will. God has bold plans for you. Being wishy-washy just won't cut it.

Are you all in? Ask God to put some unction in your gumption and give you "the want to" to want to.

Jesus said it as bluntly as can be: "I wish that you were hot or cold, but because you are lukewarm I vomit you out of my mouth" (see Rev. 3:15–16). The word here for *vomit* literally means "projectile vomit." Do you really want to live your life as a lukewarm Christian? People who ride the corral fence eventually get knocked off by an angry bull or bronc.

So pack up your saddlebags, cinch your saddle down tight, bring your oilskin duster to protect you in the heavy weather that is sure to come, and bring lots of coffee. We have work to do. We must be about our Master's business. As John Wayne would say, "No sense burning daylight." Let's ride.

What if you prayed every morning and throughout the day? What if, before every little decision, and every big one, you prayed that dangerous prayer: "Thy will be done"? Will you be the first to step forward to serve? Will you lead by example? Will you live on the edge?

I met my friend Luke Rodgers when we co-starred in a Fox TV series called *Clean Break*. My role was to mentor three young men as they pursued life-changing adventures here in Hawaii. Luke has a Scripture verse tattooed on his ribs (a very painful place for a tattoo): "I have come that you might have life and have it more abundantly" (see John 10:10). The Hawaiian pidgin translation says it this way: "I have come that you might have life and have it to da max." Are you ready for a big, heaping scoop of life with all its sorrows and joys?

Do you know that God has an adventure planned just for you? He wants to ride alongside you and be the one who goes out ahead and scouts the terrain for you. He knows the way, the pitfalls, and the great vistas before you. When the trail takes an unexpected turn, as trails always do, get ready, for the adventure begins at the detour. Trust in God. He knows the why of it all. Just ride on.

Did you know that God created you with all the gifts and the desires that you need to grow into the person who can fulfill His call? Your life adventures will be a challenge and, at times, will seem impossible, but that is where it gets good because that's when God shows up. As my mom used to say, "God is a bit of a swashbuckler, showing up at the last minute to save the day or riding in like the cavalry at the last minute. This way, we all can see that it is Him and not us that is at work."

God created you with just the right talents, desires, and limitations for your own unique quest. This life is there waiting for you to say yes or no to it. You can see that God has a plan in His design of the universe; and when you see how "fearfully and wonderfully made" you are (see Ps. 139:14), you can be sure that He has a plan for you too.

Remember, you are an arrow shot from the very heart of God. No matter the circumstances of your conception, you are not an accident. For has He not said, "Before I formed you in the womb I knew you" (Jer. 1:5)? At the moment of your conception, He infused in your body a wonderful soul with your own desires and gifts all wrapped up in a big present: God's purpose for you.

But God has given you ultimate power in the course of your life. He has given you veto power. You can say yes to God's will, or you can say no. In this way, God has made Himself subject to your will. He has given you the power to reject Him and His plan for your life.

Remember, too, that you cannot harden just a part of your heart. Be careful: when you cut God out of one area of your life, soon enough demons will come to fill that void with chaos. God is not to be trifled with. When you harden your heart to God in one area, you harden yourself to God in all areas, and your whole heart grows harder and colder. "Today, when you hear his voice, do not harden your hearts" (Heb. 3:7–8).

God honors your will. He gave you that free choice for only one reason. He gave it to you for the sake of love, for love must be given a choice. He will work with you, He will continue to knock on the door of your heart and draw you in, but He will not force Himself on you. God said, "If you are unfaithful, I am always faithful, but if you deny me, I will deny you, for I cannot deny myself" (see 2 Tim. 2:12–13).

C. S. Lewis, in *The Great Divorce*, wrote:

> There are only two kinds of people in the end: those who say to God, "Thy will be done," and those to whom God says, in the end, "Thy will be done." All that are in Hell, choose it. Without that choice there could be no Hell. No soul that seriously and constantly desires joy will ever miss it.

But you are reading this book because there is something deep down in you that affirms that God has a purpose for you and that you want to follow His plan for you, which sets you on course to happiness and the fulfillment of all desire.

As my dad used to say, "God don't make no junk." God gave you certain mental, physical, and spiritual adeptness and, along with that, certain stirrings and desires to help draw you to the unique quest that He has just for you.

But think about this. Even the limitations that you were born with or born into God uses for you to grow in virtue so that when you do move in your strengths, you do so with humility. Limitations also keep you somewhat within the navigational beacons of His will. Let's face it, some of us will just never be pole vaulters.

No matter how much you have blown it in the course of your life, don't give up. God most certainly has not given up on you. Scripture says, "The gifts and callings of God are without repentance" (see Rom. 11:29). The word *repent* means "to rethink." God is not going to rethink His intentions for you, even though you stumble and fall or get stubborn and kick against the goad.

We are all works in progress, a bit of a construction project, but remember, Jesus was a builder. Sometimes it gets depressing, and it seems as if Jesus is down in your basement just digging a bigger hole for you. But remember this: the deeper the hole, the deeper He can lay the foundation. The deeper the foundation, the taller the building He is forming. His love for you and movement in your life are relentless and are always for your good.

We like to call Jesus "Lord." But what do we really mean by "Lord"? Are we ready for God to put His own detours or even roadblocks in our paths? How often now, when you look back at things you wanted to go a certain way and they didn't, and it made your life harder and more confusing, how often do you now say, "Thank You, God, for helping me dodge that bullet. I see that Your way is, as we say in Hawaii, 'mo bettah.'"

Keep reminding yourself that no matter where you got off track, God has a portal, a window, right there where you are, that you can leap through to get back to the path of virtue, where God will meet you and guide you on a step-by-step pursuit of the adventure of His will. Virtue is not a far-off goal. Right now, you can make a decision to act in virtue that, in time, will become a habit.

When you are living in God's will, when you are under the spout where His blessings come out, you get to see God do stuff and you get to enter into that stuff with Him. As my friend Jason Jones likes to say, it is the "Holy Spirit Action Plan."

Certainly, we may fail. We surfers know this. We fall more than little children. Failing is part of growing and learning. We have to give ourselves permission to fail before we can succeed.

Certainly, there is a real risk in failing, there is danger in a wipeout, but do you know what is even more dangerous? Just sitting on the beach and letting life pass us by. In Hawaii, we call people who dress like surfers but never paddle out on big days *posers*.

You see, big-wave riders do not have a death wish: they have a life wish—that is, they have a desire to live life to the full, just as Luke's tattoo says.

If you find that your life is just cruising along smoothly, and you keep making and reaching your goals but you still feel a certain emptiness, you are perhaps in a more dangerous place. You are living too deep inside your comfort zone. Everything seems as if it is just rolling along according to your plan, but what if you died tonight? Thomas à Kempis wrote that death always seems to come sooner than we think. And then we are gone; we are so quickly forgotten. Someone else takes our place, and life closes in around the memory of us, and so we become a distant memory and are oh so quickly forgotten.

When life is easy, lethargy and selfishness can creep in, and it is so easy to forget our *Memento mori* Code. This is the danger of a life squandered. So then, how do we move on from being just adrift to blazing new trails? How do we know and pursue God's will?

When I graduated from Baylor University, and my new adventure in life was about to begin, my mom told me that God had given her a kind of a vision for me. God had taken me to a big window and opened it wide with a beautiful vista of mountains and streams opening out before me. All of these different places were opportunities that I could pursue. His word to her for me was this: "I have given you many gifts and talents, and your heart is with me. Look out and pick any one of these, any one that you desire, and I will bless you as you pursue it. Choose and know that it is my will for you."

This spoke to me of the liberty of the freedom of choice that God gives each of us, but, in a more mysterious way, I also knew that God placed desires in my heart, and following them would set me on the path of His will. I knew that among all those possibilities, there was just that "one thing" that God had prepared for me to pursue. Somehow I would just *know* to choose that one, because God is like that.

God clearly says that He has a plan for you, but that plan can only be entered into by entering into friendship with Him. Think of it this way: He did not give Abraham a map to the Holy Land. He said, "Pack up your stuff, get your camels ready, and go to the land that I will show you." Abe walked day by day with God as He showed him the way. And remember, God called Abraham His friend. Being on adventure with God does that. It was on the trail, riding our motorcycles together in a pack on *Long Ride Home*, that the men on the ride became friends.

Aristotle and Aquinas both wrote that desiring happiness is good; it is seeking our telos. Happiness is found in fulfilling and perfecting the true natural good that comes with your unique nature, your personal telos, your true end, your true purpose, which God has just for you. Do you recall that Jesus taught us to pursue happiness? When He taught us the Beatitudes, He prefaced each one by saying, "Happy are you when ..."

The noblest among us are the courageously happy ones in pursuit of virtue and God's will.

It is only in God that we are perfected and find happiness. You know, Jesus commands us to "be perfect, as your heavenly Father is perfect" (Matt. 5:48). Pretty gnarly commandment! But do you remember Jesus using that "be" command somewhere else? How about when He commanded "Let there *be* light"? By His word, He created the universe. So it is when Jesus said, "Be perfect." This is not only a command: it is actually a creative word of grace. As you abide in Christ and cooperate with His grace, He will perfect you.

A salmon, by its nature, swims upstream; an eagle soars to new heights. So do you, by your God-given nature—by your very essence—spread the wings of your soul and soar to God.

What if you were an eagle and never knew you could fly or were afraid to take that first leap out of your aerie and into thin air? You were meant to soar much higher than your nest and see vistas that man has never dreamed of. What if you were meant to dive in a streamlined streak or soar above the storm higher and faster than any other bird, but instead you spent your time trying to hide huddled under your mediocrity in a cold rain? That is not your telos. There is no joy in the sweet self-pity and comfort of mediocrity.

What if God had a plan for your life and you just kinda-sorta went for it?

I remember my first big jump, my first big leap of faith. I was only about five years old. My dad set me on the roof of our garage as he worked on the rain gutters. Then he stretched out his arms and said, "Jump." To me, that roof was a mile high. I was so scared. But I edged myself forward; then I crouched and reached for my father and jumped. It was the greatest thrill of my life. And practically before I'd even made the leap, he caught me.

The point is this: to really live the life that God has for us, we have to leap. I had to make a choice: Trust my dad or not trust him. Go or not go. There was no going halfway. I wonder what my life would have been like if I had not learned to jump and trust at that moment. I would have chosen fear instead of trust, and how sad my whole life would have been if I remained in that mindset.

I remember my first jump out of an airplane. I had taken an accelerated freefall course so that when I jumped, I did not have to be attached to my jumpmaster. The door opened, and it was time. Go or no go.

You can't kinda-sorta jump out of a plane. You make a choice. Go or don't go. I remember once taking my son Jeremiah for his first jump. We waited until the other dozen jumpers exited because I wanted to jump out right after my son and then hang out with him for a while in the sky. The whole plane emptied out except for Jeremiah, his jumpmaster, me, and another new jumper and his jumpmaster. Just before we were to jump, the plane had to make a long, two-minute circle back to the jump zone, and the adrenaline was amping through us.

Then, suddenly, the plane filled with a horrible stench. The other jumper had lost his courage and lost control of his bowels. He never did jump. He sat in his own excrement all the way back to the runway with the plane. How tragic! He missed out on the rush of a lifetime. Don't be that person who does not take that leap of faith into God's will. Don't stink up the place, wallowing in doubt and the lethargy of mediocrity, looking for an excuse to fail.

Faith leaps.

It requires a certain prudence and boldness, but ultimately, if you are a Christian, you are, by definition, called to be bold. When a first-time jumper lands, all the other jumpers smile and shake his hand and say the same thing to him: "Welcome to the sky!" And you feel, at the moment, that you can do anything that you set your mind to.

Be the person to whom Jesus says, "Welcome to the sky!"

What is the adventure that seems to be beckoning to you right now? Is it asking that girl out on a date—or asking her to marry you? Is it deciding to change from a full-time job to a part-time job so you can go to that trade school that you keep thinking about? Is it joining a Crossfit gym? Is it starting a business? Is it writing a book? Is it running for the school board or teaching catechism? Is it starting a men's group? What is it? Maybe it is even skydiving. Yikes!

Is this a time for resting or trusting? The choice is yours.

Many reading this may be a bit older, and they may feel that they are drawing to the end of their opportunity for adventure. They never pushed the airplane engine to full throttle, never reached rotation speed, never pulled back on the wheel in the cockpit, never felt the nose lift up as the ground falls away. Many opportunities were presented to them, but they aborted those adventures and now realize that much of their life is behind them and they squandered it in mediocrity or selfish, pointless ambition.

Does that describe you? If so, God isn't finished with you yet.

"Your youth is renewed like the eagle's" (Ps. 103:5). You see, an eagle, as it reaches beyond its midlife, becomes more and more weak and vulnerable. Its wings have become tattered from all the wear and tear, and its beak has become a bit crusted over. It cannot hunt or eat as well as it could in its youth. So it is weak. Can you imagine being so powerful and then becoming vulnerable like that? Or maybe you feel a bit like that right now.

During this eagle's midlife crisis, something amazing happens. It flies to its aerie, away from danger, and it just isolates itself and waits. In time, its tattered feathers begin to fall off as it molts. The eagle is not able to hunt, and so it becomes weaker and weaker as death seems to knock at its door. The eagle cowers under the rainstorms and looks bleakly below as life passes it by.

Have you ever experienced this in your life? Have you ever found yourself floundering and vulnerable in a hopeless, pointless malaise—a time of molting, when you have reached a dead end in your career or in a relationship, or a financial reversal, or maybe a health challenge?

God is not finished with you yet.

You see, something wonderful happens to that eagle. In time, new feathers grow in and push out all the old feathers, and the eagle is ready to spread its wings again. God renews its youth. This time, though, it is ready to embrace its life more than ever because it appreciates now what it means to spread its wings and fly.

When the next big storm arrives, the eagle does not cower beneath the onslaught. Instead, it flies out to meet the storm and uses the storm's powerful updrafts to lift itself higher than it has ever flown before. It soars higher and higher until, at some point, the change in air pressure breaks off the crustiness on its beak. It is now as powerful as a youthful eagle—but, better yet, it has all that vitality *plus* all the savvy and skill developed over the years as a hunter and provider. Its youth is renewed.

As you get older and (hopefully) wiser, God has a plan and a vision for you. Moses and Abraham were both over seventy-five when God called them. You are more skilled, gifted, and experienced than ever in your life. This is no time to put yourself on a shelf. It is time to say yes to God and impact the lives of those around you.

In his nineties, my dad could no longer serve at the altar as a deacon, but he sat in his wheelchair near the back entrance of the church and blessed each child as they came by, telling them just how special they were and how God made them so beautiful and unique. And he would give them holy cards. The children adored him. And they found out just how loved and how special they were to God. He would say, "God made you just the way you are and He loves you. You are so special." Their parents took his message to heart too.

So, wherever you find yourself right now, what is your telos? What is your purpose, your true end?

The early Church called themselves the people of the Way. Do you see? They were on a journey. They were on a quest. They were on an adventure. They were on a trail drive of their own. They were on the Way. Are you?

Time to mount up and ride the Proving Trail.

I've noticed ... that whenever a man is asked to be realistic he is being asked to betray something in which he believes. It is the favorite argument of those who believe that only the ends matter, not the means.

—Louis L'Amour, *How the West Was Won*

Rule 7

Ride the Proving Trail: Pursue Your Course of Action

A man has to blaze his own trail.
—Louis L'Amour, *Ride the River*

When I was twenty years old, I discovered a twenty-six-hundred-year-old quote that set something solid in me and stirred something powerful up in me too. I felt like a racehorse seething with power, hardly able to control his anticipation as he waits for the rider to spur him into action and release him to his desire to run. The verse says, "Write the vision; make it plain on tablets, so he may run who reads it.... If it seems slow, wait for it; it will surely come" (Hab. 2:2–3). It speaks about a runner, a courier who is to run from town to town and proclaim a great victory.

This verse set me on a course blazing my own trail, riding the proving trail—a trail that would test me and teach me. I felt like a high-strung thoroughbred horse in the starting gate, impatiently raising its head and shaking its mane, with its feet pawing the ground. I set goals, and as soon as the gates opened, I was in hot pursuit. Sometimes my goals were a bit bodacious, and I bit off more than I could chew, but I took off running, and I have never looked back.

The sheer joy of running the race should propel us toward our goals.

The biblical words I just quoted were written by an obscure Old Testament prophet whose name, "Habakkuk," means "to embrace," "to clinch," or "to grapple."

Are you ready to embrace God's vision for you? Are you ready to clinch it and grapple your way through it? Because if you do that, your life will be a wild adventure, and your actions and your virtue will proclaim Christ's victory. The vision of Habakkuk spoke of hope of the coming victory in the midst of darkness and chaos. He speaks to us now that very same message of victory. He exhorts us to have the boldness to clinch with God, even to grapple with Him, until that wrestling with Him becomes an embrace with Him—and to come to grips with His unique, gnarly, and wild plan that He has just for us. All God wants is for us to get real with Him—to lay it all out on the line. God wants us to wrestle with Him; it is Him "to whom we must give account" (see Heb. 4:13). Even to say no to Him, to resist Him, but never letting go of Him, until finally, in all the muck and mud of our stubborn lives, His relentless love breaks through and fills our souls with "new and right desires" (see Ezek. 36:26) and all we can say to Him is "Yes, Father. Your will be done."

Say yes to Him now as He reorients your disordered, direction-less, chaotic life into a relentless pursuit of the wild adventure of His will. Say yes to Him as He takes you from the bland everyday-ness of a life tethered to the hitching post of lethargy, mediocrity, and self-pity and puts you on a path to the bold *coraggio* of His purpose, His path, and His plan for your life. You are meant for this wild ride. Now the time has come. Mount up and ride.

When I was about nineteen years old, I had a powerful conversion experience in Christ, and my love for Him just overflowed like the streams that the prophet Joel talked about. So it was natural for everyone around me to start pressing me about becoming a priest. My desire had been to get married and to be a father. But I was not sure what God wanted, and so the grappling began. It was scary. It became harder and harder for me to call Him "Lord" because I worried that He wanted me to be a priest. Finally, I went on a seven-day fast and then a ten-hour drive from Waco, Texas, to Pecos, New Mexico, to a Benedictine Monastery. (I am now an oblate at a sister monastery they planted here in O'ahu.)

The first day at the monastery, I was miserable. I was still not able to say yes to God. Finally, as I agonized in my room that night, tossing and turning and wrestling with God, I was able to say, "God, as hard as it is to serve You, it is harder *not* to. I will serve you as a priest if that is Your will." Finally, my soul had rest. God had His answer from me, and though I did not have His reply as to His will for me, I had that rest that only comes from abiding in His will.

Two months later, I found myself driving my little yellow VW Bug all the way back up to the same area, but this time to a seminary in Santa Fe, New Mexico. On my first morning there, I woke up ready to discover God's will. If only I knew what that was! I met some great seminarians and even attended class with them. But that afternoon I hiked up Mon de Sol—the Mountain of the Sun—and I prayed in anguish: *I am willing to do Your will, God. But what is Your will?*

Finally, after an hour of prayer, the answer came as clear as a bell. The words rang in my heart from God. "Well—what do you want?"

My response was: "I want to be married; I want to be a father."
Then, right away, the verse came to me: "Delight yourself in the
LORD, and He will give you the desires of your heart" (Ps. 37:4).
Then came God's assurance. "Don't you know that it is I who
gave you those desires, who planted those desires in you? And I
will also fulfill them."

This is the kind of grappling that God wants us to do with
Him, like Jacob wrestling with God in the desert. When a fighter
is losing, he closes distance and clinches so that his opponent's
fists don't hurt so much because he cannot get a full swing. Jacob
told the Lord on that long, dark night that he would not let go
until the Lord blessed him.

So wrestle it out with God. Get real. Have it out with Him.
A little blood, sweat, and tears is a lot more real than sweet, neutered self-excusing, "I'm sorry, I must have not heard you right.
You could not be calling me to heroic virtue and self-donation.
You could not be calling me to that wild adventure of Your will.
You could not be calling me to pursue that goal and that plan
and to grow so that I can become that purpose. I have other,
less important, less fruitful things to do, like yelling at the news
every night and watching football on Sunday."

When God gave Habakkuk that message, He was like a general sending a messenger — a *runner*, as they were called — to run
from battlefield to battlefield, from village to village, never stopping as he shouts loudly, announcing the news of a great victory.
That is our role in life, is it not? We're supposed to carry that
message of victory, to stay the course even when things get tough,
even if the victory seems delayed and so far away. We are called
to be that man who sets the course of action and stays the course
with relentless courage and bold action.

We are meant to ride the proving trail.

A month ago, my son and his wife took my bride and me to a special showing of the movie *Napoleon Dynamite*. The actors who played Napoleon, Pedro, and Uncle Rico were there. After the show, we got to talk with them. I even got to play catch with Uncle Rico, using the football that I brought for him to sign.

In the movie, Pedro's promise to the student body when he ran for school president was that their "wildest dreams would come true." I pray that same way for my bride every morning. "God, I pray that Cindy's wildest dreams will come true." I pray this prayer confidently, knowing that I am in line with God's will, for there is a promise that says God will "give us new and right desires" (see Ezek. 36:26). You see, if you ask God to plant those wildest dreams in you, He will, and He'll give them water and sunshine and make them grow strong and straight and tall.

God is wild, and He has wild dreams that are only for you, that are meant only for you to fulfill. If you think you can tame God, take a quick look at a quasar or a black hole or a dinosaur. If you think you have been able to keep God inside your little comfortable box that you put on your shelf, ask yourself why you are inwardly frustrated, angry, and depressed. Could it mean you are missing out on your telos, your purpose, and its accompanying happiness?

In all of this, remember, God's ultimate purpose for any goal that He gives you is for you to become like His Son. We were made in God's image—we are the *imago Dei*—in that we were given a spiritual, rational soul, which can commune with God. But we are not always very much like Him. Our race lost our original innocence in the Fall a long, long time ago.

So wipe the slate clean. Push the reset button. Take a fresh look at everything, and let's start anew, "for like the dewfall, His mercies are new every morning" (Lam. 3:22–23). Every morning is a fresh start. Begin today. My dad had this embarrassing habit of saying to random people, like the girl at the checkout counter, "Happy birthday." (I always knew it was coming, so I would just kind of sneak away.) When they looked up, sort of perplexed, he would just say, "Happy birthday. This is the first day of the rest of your life."

So, on this first day of the rest of your life, here is how to create and pursue a plan:

Step 1: *Write your dreams out.* These are not goals yet. These are just dreams, inklings in your heart. Open up your heart, expand your vision, and look at all the possibilities that your gifts and desires draw you to. Be sure to write down even your crazy ones. Pedro would. Sometimes, hidden in those crazy dreams is the gem that God is really calling you to.

Before you begin, remember to pray the most dangerous prayer that a man can pray. You know what it is: "Thy will be done." Jesus is our Trail Boss. He has a plan, and He knows the way. This isn't His first rodeo. Just pray, "Lord, I'm riding for Your brand. I'm all in, come hell or high water. Show me that path that I have neglected, that I've been too blind to see. Show me the trail I should ride, and give me a good horse, and I will ride it. I abandon myself to the wild adventure of Your will."

Then grab a pad of paper and a pencil (my dad used to say that only God writes in pen) and write. Write as fast as a gunfighter draws his guns and fires. With both guns blazing, write down your hopes, your aspirations, your big goals, your small goals, your silly goals, your out-of-control, crazy-wild goals. Write each one down before your doubt catches up to you and shoots them down like a sniper on the roof of the Long Branch Saloon. Fill a page, then another, then another. Your Creed and your Code will lead you to your goals. Let that horse run.

Write about your career, your fitness, your desire for adventure, and your woman, whether you have even met her or not. Write about where you want to travel, the next skill set you want to develop, your quest for knowledge. Write about how you can lead, how you can serve, how you intend to strike the purest gold of the richest vein—that is, the mother lode of personal time with God.

Imagine what is just over the next hill and even what is beyond the horizon. Lean forward in the saddle, slap leather, and tell your imagination, "Giddyup! Let's ride!" Then let it run wild.

Now, before you finish, remember, I said dare to write down even your wildest dreams.

I have always had the habit of doing just this. I have volumes of leather books with my hurriedly scribbled notes on once-blank pages. I jot down thoughts, turns of phrase, inspirations, and spiritual insights. I write down dreams that I begin to hold in expectation, to be discerned over time, that perhaps will become goals. The other day, as I rearranged my bookshelves, I glanced through some of these old journals. It was shocking to me to realize just how many of my ponderings, wonderings, and wanderings that I had so casually jotted down had, in time, become goals that were set, pursued, and accomplished.

These goals begin, quite often, with what might be a sort of nudge from the Holy Spirit, although sometimes it can be more of a shove. As I got better at understanding and following these inklings from the Lord, I got to the point where it just seems as if I know the next thing that the Spirit is leading me to. I don't know the whole picture, but I kind of know the next step.

There are times when we may experience a great discontent. It is time to ask ourselves, "Is this because I am not dealing with my current circumstances properly? Are there things that I need to do to set things right in my life—things that I am just not doing? Am I not properly caring for my present *kuleana*, my stewardship, my God-given responsibility?

Or could this be the Holy Spirit leading me in a new direction?

Perhaps, in this situation, God has lifted His grace from me because it's time to break camp and move on. One of the dangers in life is to get stuck in a rut. God may have led you into that situation, but He may now be leading you onward and saying, "Behold, I do a new thing" (see Rev. 21:5). "Follow me." He led you there and gave you the grace to be there, but perhaps only for a season. So we don't want to get stuck like a wagon wheel in a muddy rut.

I felt this in a big way when I was living a comfortable life in Southern California and running my successful CPA firm. One day, I just got the feeling of "been there, done that, got the postcard. Next?" The cloud had lifted like a June fog. It was time to move on. So I sold my big CPA firm in California and moved to Hawaii. It was the right thing at the right time.

Think of it this way. When the children of Israel sojourned with Moses in the wilderness, God's Spirit led them with a cloud by day and a pillar of fire at night. When the Holy Spirit rested, they knew it was time to set up camp and pitch the temple — or, as they called it, the "Tent of Meeting" — in the wilderness. I like that. It was where they would meet with God, where they hung out with God and, as we say in Hawaii, "talked story." They might be there for a day, a month, or longer, but then, one day, the cloud would just suddenly lift up from the tent. Then it was time to pack up and move and follow the cloud.

By the way, on the march, the singers and worshippers went first. That is the way we are to pursue God's will too. We are to "enter His gates with thanksgiving, and His courts with praise" (Ps. 100:4). We are not to grumble and complain, like some of them in the desert who ended up being swallowed up when the earth took a big gulp. We are to "give thanks in all circumstances" (1 Thess. 5:18) — yes, even when the tire goes flat; yes, even when the bull has broken down the fence again; yes, even when there is no surf. Praise Him in all things. Praising is how we enter into God's presence — not grumbling, not whining, not complaining as if God doesn't know what He is doing.

There are times in our lives when we sense that the grace that God had given us to do a certain thing, or live in a certain place, or serve a certain cause, just seems to lift from our shoulders. We need to recognize that God is on the move. When you sense that God is not giving you the grace to move in a certain direction, look up for the cloud of the Holy Spirit, to see whether He is leading you in a new way.

There are times when God does more than give us that peaceful sense or a nudge. Sometimes He uses our circumstances to give us a good push. He squeezes us out of our circumstances like a tube of toothpaste. He gets us moving. (Remember, you give Him the right to do this when you call Him "Lord.")

Not long ago, I was having coffee with my bride and I heard myself say, "I think I'm done riding motorcycles and filming *Long Ride Home*."

She looked at me and nodded and said, "Yes. Please." She, too, felt that the cloud of grace had been lifted. That particular work was accomplished, and God was up to something new. Somehow, that unquenchable desire to hit the road with the pack and roam the whole country while filming our TV show was just gone.

Not long after that decision was made, an old inspiration that I had sensed back about the time we chose to launch *Long Ride*

Home resurfaced. Before we started filming our motorcycle show, we had also considered filming sailing adventures in the Caribbean and showing our life in Hawaii and using that cinematic adventure to draw people into our teaching experiences with God. Could it be that this was a vision, like the one Habakkuk spoke of, that had tarried? Was it now time to pursue it? I have next to me on my desk right now a new blue three-ring binder labeled *Adventure in Paradise*. We shall see.

Cindy and I are praying about pursuing this as we discover and test the water to see if this nudge is from the Lord. It is time to pray this "Holy Spirit Action Plan" into existence.

After Elijah had battled the priests and prophets of Baal on Mount Carmel—after he had won the people over to the service of the true God—it was time for him to pray. God had caused a great drought for many years; now that this confrontation was over, it was time for Elijah to pray for rain. It is God's will to send rain, but not without our participating in prayer.

When he prayed, he squatted down in the same position that women in those days took when they gave birth. He was giving birth to a vision. Seven times he prayed for the vision for God to send rain to come to pass in the same way that a woman goes through rounds of birth pangs. Finally, a small cloud, about the size of a man's hand, appeared. He continued to pray until finally the rain came down like a river.

When God gives us a vision, we, too, need to give birth to that vision. We need to participate with God and *pray* that vision into existence.

These inspirations from the Holy Spirit, these goals, seem to come to me at random times; sometimes they come to me while I am out riding my motorcycle or surfing, but mostly they come to me either during morning prayer, awakened by a hot cup of coffee, or perhaps in the evening when I'm reading and having a whiskey and a cigar, as I am doing at this moment.

By the way, I drink my whiskey straight, not diluted by even a melting ice cube. I keep it cold with frozen bullets. Do not dilute your dreams with lack of faith. Make them targets that you pursue with the precision and resolve of a well-aimed bullet.

Step 2: *Discern and choose which dreams should become goals.* The next step, after jotting down your thoughts in a journal, is to ponder them for a while—maybe for a day or two but no longer than a week. Then start to discern which ones are worthy of you, which ones bring you a sense of peace and rightness, which ones you are drawn to. Which one will cause you to grow in its pursuit? Start to ride through them the same way a cowboy rides through a herd on his cutting horse, separating the good cattle from the rest of the herd. Choose the ones that you want to pursue and begin to turn them into concrete goals, each with its own plan of action, always being sure that they align with each other.

That is when I set my leather journal next to a blue three-ring binder. I label it and put half a dozen dividers in it to categorize what I find out as I go through my discovery, and in time, I use that notebook to chart my course.

No need to waste your time pursuing the trivial. No need pursuing something that you are not drawn to. Don't waste your life away. Set your course and start now. When I rode my bicycle across the United States, from time to time a mad dog would come out and try to chase me down. Once, I had to kick that mad dog to the curb. Don't let that mad dog of doubt, worry, and feeling unworthy chase you down.

As you look, keep in mind your unique "gifts and callings of God as well as your Creed and your Code;" choose your goals.

What is it that you do that you sense is pleasing to God? What is consistent with your skills and desires? What is consistent with your telos, the fulfillment of your unique nature.

Choose your goals with the knowledge that Jesus is with you in the process. Just like on the schoolyard football field, it was Jesus who first chose you to be on His team. "You did not choose me, but I chose you ... that you should ... bear fruit" (John 15:16). Then He draws a play out in the dirt and smiles at you and says, "Go long."

You see, Jesus is a planner. Just look at the intricate plan of the universe. Thirteen billion years ago, He unleashed the heavens so that one day you would be born. The Bible says, "In all your ways acknowledge him, and He will direct your steps" (Prov. 3:6). "I know the plans I have for you" (Jer. 29:11). So, in all of your planning, seek God and His plan first.

Now is the time for action, not excuses. If you are not happy with things as they are, ask yourself, "When will I stop being blameless and blameful? When will I stop playing the victim, faulting others or my circumstances for my situation in life? At some point, I have to own up to the fact that my present circumstances are the result of a lot of small and big decisions in my past, such as when I chose the comfortableness of self-pity and laziness and mediocrity—when I lacked grit and failed to choose the good."

My dad used to say, "Little Billy did not get to choose whether his dad was a bank president or a bank robber, but he can choose his response to that, and he can now choose his own course." Regardless of your circumstances, you can become a decisive man of virtue whose pursuit of success brings others along with you. You are not a victim. Stop blaming the circumstances that you were born into. Build. Starting now, right where you are, build.

Where you are today is the result of a lot of small decisions. Start making proper choices now. Make every choice count, and see where you are two days from now, two years from now.

The difference between God's will and your own vain pursuit is frustration, anxiety, and lack of joy. It is time to move on from just getting along. It is time to move on from just passing through life to the joy of blazing a new trail, led by God in the service of God. He will find pleasure in your doing it, and you will find fulfillment.

Step 3: *Now chart a specific course for those goals one at a time.* As you do this, choose the good. Choose goals that are greater than you can accomplish with your current skill set and knowledge. Choose something you cannot do without growing in virtue—that you cannot do without God's help. In this way, a goal is more like something you *become* than something you accomplish. Choose a goal that champions a cause, that is greater than yourself. Remember that your decisions today are a time machine to your future.

Consider, more deeply, just one specific dream. Discern again: Is God in it? What is the goal of the goal? Or put it another way: What is the *why* of accomplishing this thing? Is it consistent with God's purpose for your life? Is it consistent with your Creed and your Code? Will pursuing it result in fractured energy, or does it align with your other goals, like Robin Hood's arrow, that flies through the air and hits the target, splitting the shaft of the last arrow that he shot? Is it worthy of your pursuit? Will it bless your *ohana* and those you are called to serve? What will be the good and the bad if you do this? Perhaps, more importantly, what will be the good and the bad if you *don't* pursue this?

Once you have gone through that thought process, ask whether this goal gives you a sense of peace and rightness. Will this goal bring balance to your family life and your work life? Will it encourage rest and play and good health? Will it help you to serve others? Will it draw you closer to God? Do your goals flow together like a good day of surf with clean waves rolling in like corduroy from the horizon? Or are they disjointed and confused, bouncing into each other like a bunch of raw recruits learning to march?

Scripture says, "Seek peace, pursue it" (Ps. 34:14). As you think about which direction to take and what decision to make, do you feel the inner peace that marks the presence of the Holy Spirit? This is not looking at the outward difficulties that the goal will entail. It's not unlike the Holy Spirit to lead you on a path that requires boldness and faith to face many challenges. Don't worry if it seems full of challenges; just check in with God. Just lean in and ask your Friend, the Holy Spirit: "Is this You?"

There is a peace that comes from winning a battle. There is a peace that comes when things are set in order. But there is a peace that only the Holy Spirit brings, a "peace that surpasses all understanding" (Phil. 4:7). Do you sense that peace of God as you write down your goal?

Then simply pray that dangerous prayer of Jesus: "Thy will be done."

When we ask God to show us His will, the Lord's voice will speak to us in many ways. I have been to the cave on the island of Patmos where God's voice crackled like lightning and thunder with so much power that it split the rock of the cave above the apostle John's head in three long lines. It was then that the voice of God revealed His plans for the end times.

God's voice shouted loudly to the apostle Paul on the road to Damascus. It knocked him off his high horse as Paul kicked against the goad of God's will like a stubborn mule. Then, when Paul was humbled and when he humbled himself, Jesus told Paul

His plans for him. Scripture promises, "And your ears shall hear a word behind you, saying, 'This is the way, walk in it,' when you turn to the right or when you turn to the left" (Isa. 30:21). So even though we men are sometimes stubborn, and we have selective hearing and are set in our ways, if we ask Him to speak to us, God will make His ways known to us.

The apostles also heard God's voice like thunder when, at Christ's baptism, the Father said, "This is my beloved Son. Listen to Him" (see Mark 1:11; 9:7). So we must learn to listen.

Sometimes God speaks loudly, as when there is an abrupt change in our circumstances that gets our attention. More often, though, He speaks to us in a "still, small voice" (see 1 Kings 19:12) that we hear only when we lean in to God in prayer. John heard God's voice like thunder in the cave at Patmos. But there is another cave. There is the one that Elijah fled to after his great victory. He was depressed and cried out to God for help. First there came a mighty wind, thunder, and rain. But the Bible says God was not in those things. It was only when everything became still and quiet that God spoke.

Keep in mind that this moment of great self-doubt and depression in Elijah's life came *after* he accomplished a great victory. He felt that he was alone and had no purpose anymore. So he ran a long, long way away. Some say hundreds of miles away, across the desert, as far as Sinai, and he hid out in a cave from everyone else—even God.

But then God came to him and gave him a good talking to. He cajoled him more than consoled him. He challenged him to stop being full of self-pity. Then He told him, "Brush yourself off and get going. I've got a job for you." God sent him on a mission.

If you find yourself doubting God or yourself, get up and get to work. God has a mission for you; He will lead you as you get in motion. You know what you need to do. You may not know the whole plan, but you know what you need to do next. Do it.

God does not speak in a monotone. His vision isn't cast in black and white. Don't limit God, or put Him in a box, or place Him on a shelf. God has a rich, bright, clear, colorful vision for you. He has a path for you to follow on your adventure, an adventure only you can live. As the saying goes, "Your future's so bright you have to wear shades."

Men: pay close attention here. That still, small voice in which God is speaking to you may just be the loving, discerning voice of your bride. Listen to her. Travel the path of her wisdom. She has secret places with the Lord that often only a woman can know. She possesses subtlety and intuition that a man, made out of mud and clay, may just miss. Her ways will not always make sense—until, suddenly, they do. Listen to her.

Throughout the day, I have learned to ask Cindy for her thoughts and her prayers. God answers almost immediately when she lifts up her heart to Him in silent prayers, for He is "drawn to her gentle and contrite heart." God listens to your bride. Do you?

My mom used to say, "If there is a choice between two paths, choose the harder one." I think another way to say that is: choose the one that requires more boldness. Yes, prudence would have you listen to your fear. Ponder just what the hazards are on this path. Develop strategies to overcome them. But then pull the trigger.

I think God really digs on a man who comes out with both guns blazing.

When you are seeking God's will and provision, don't forget to ask Jesus' Mom, Mary, to pray for you. Remember, she was the one who kick-started Jesus' public ministry at the wedding in Cana. She definitely has her Son's attention. Ask her to intercede for you.

As we were filming season 1 of *Long Ride Home*, when we crossed the border into Louisiana, we were met by members of the Catholic Cross Bearers Motorcycle Ministry. We rode up and got off our motorcycles, and we all stood facing each other. It reminded me of the shootout at the OK Corral. With cameras rolling, I heard myself say, "Show us your weapons." It was so cool because each one of them reached into their vest pocket and pulled out their own rosary. For us men, that should be our weapon of choice. We need to listen and pray to our Mother to intercede for us.

Step 4: *Plan your course of action.* Now it is time to write down each goal and write down a specific course of action. My dad always told me that the difference between a daydreamer and a real man is that a man writes his dreams down and turns them into goals and a plan of action. Goals activate faith along the path of God's will. So write each one down. Remember Habakkuk: " Write the vision . . . so he may run who reads it." It's time to run.

Write it specifically with a target date. What will be the waypoints along the way? What will be the obstacles that you will have to grow to overcome and the actions you will have to take to get through them? How will you measure your progress? Some goals lend themselves to metrics. It is helpful—even fun—and you can keep score. For example, I used a Garmin watch for two decades to keep score on my weekly walking and paddling distance goals. Now I use a Fitbit because it gives so much more information.

Unless you have a plan, you are just going in circles.

I remember hunting in the remote, rugged mountains of Montana next to Glacier Park, in an area that I was not familiar with. Four of us split up on foot and began to walk through more than a foot of fresh snow along a mountain canyon with the plan of meeting at the top, near a fire road. The day started out sunny, but then the clouds came in and covered the mountain peaks. It was hard to get my bearings, so I pulled out my new mountaineering compass and used it to guide my steps.

The compass was new, yet the reading just didn't make sense. I went by my own "dead" reckoning, and I was relieved when I eventually came across a set of fresh tracks left by another hunter. I was saved. I figured that he must know the way. So I followed them up along ridgelines around trees and up a small canyon until I came across another set of tracks. As I studied the trail, I realized that one person had set the trail and then another had come along and followed it. I scratched my head and looked at my surroundings until it suddenly dawned on me. I had been running around in circles following my own dead reckoning was certainly leading me on a path to death. Because of the low clouds and the inability to see the sun or the mountain peaks for guidance I took out my compass and forced myself to follow it. An hour later, I came out on the fire road and met up with the other men.

Without a plan, without a compass, our lives are just going in circles.

Years ago, I pulled out a three-ring binder and put a label on its spine that read "Cross-Country Bicycle Ride." I inserted some papers in the rings and then wrote on the top of the first page: "Bicycle Ride — Spring 2001." I set up tabs and labeled them "Route," "Equipment," "Training," "Financing" and "Fundraising." I spaced them with plenty of paper between for each category. I use the binder's front sleeve as an in-basket for things that came my way that I needed to deal with. As I dealt with these items, I placed each behind the proper divider. For example, behind one of the dividers was a highway map of the United

States with a red line tracing a possible route from the beach in San Diego to the beach in Jacksonville, Florida. In time, that section was filled with strategic stops that I would make along the way. I use the binder's back sleeve as my out-basket for things that I need to take with me and do.

Starting that notebook made that goal spring to life. Before I knew it, my daughter agreed to drive my escort truck. Within six months, we were off on our twenty-five-hundred-mile, twenty-seven-days adventure. Seventeen years later, I would retrace that same course in reverse on my motorcycle as we filmed our first season of *Long Ride Home*.

I knew that starting that notebook was a dangerous act. It was like loading bullets in a revolver with all six cylinders chambered and no empty cylinder for safety. That notebook was now potent with energy and movement. Things could get out of hand pretty fast. I know that once I activate a blue notebook for a new goal, that it somehow begins to take on a life of its own. I would become more aware of information coming my way that might be useful. I would accidentally bump into people who could help me as the Holy Spirit Action Plan kicked in. The gears and wheels in my mind would begin spinning, and they'd go on spinning even when I was asleep. Sometimes I would wake up with a thought, a question, or an inspiration to jot down in the notebook.

I did the same thing when I launched my CPA firm, when I pursued my Masters Degree, and when I trained for years to obtain my Ninja Black Belt. I did the same for planning my betrothal to Cindy on Santorini, for obtaining my first sailboat and learning to sail, for getting my pilot license with my fifteen-year-old son Joshua, for training for the first tandem-surfing world title in Australia, for building that cabin in Montana with my family, for selling my CPA firm and moving to Hawaii, for starting the radio show and launching the TV show, and, of course, for writing my first book—as well as the book you're reading now.

Write your goals down big enough so that you can run while reading and let God lead you as He puts you in motion.

Step 5: *Move.* As Captain Jack Sparrow said "Now, bring me that horizon." Start to move toward the goal that you have discerned and have a sense that it is God's will. Your goal will come to you as you go to it, for God is with you. You are on an adventure with God.

If you don't move, how can He direct you if you are at a dead stop?

When I was young, a lot of cars did not have power steering. It was so hard to turn that steering wheel when the car was standing still, but once it got rolling, it was easy. I have laid my motorcycle down only twice, once when I was going about three miles an hour inside Diamond Head Crater and then again when I was at a full stop near the Makapu'u lighthouse. If we are not moving or if we are moving slowly and tentatively without faith, how can God guide us? Once we start moving, He can direct our path. Why would He say that His "word is a lamp unto our feet" if He did not intend us to be moving (see Ps. 119:105)?

As we move, God can steer us toward certain waypoints. He can even adjust our course a bit and take us around some obstacles, over some, and through others. Remember, obstacles are not walls. They are launching ramps. On every trail drive, there is that scout who goes on ahead of everyone else to search out the easiest path that offers water and the most grass and water. So, as you pursue your goal. Be prepared for God to go out ahead of you and perhaps adjust your direction.

You see, God wants us to walk with Him on our adventure. That is a huge part of why He sets out the adventure for us in the first place. God did not give Abraham a detailed map. He just said, "Go to the place that I will show you." Abraham had to check in with God every day so that he could know and do God's will. In this way, Abraham became a friend of God.

When we start to film each season of *Long Ride Home*, I pray and seek out what the Lord wants the general theme to be. Since it is an immersive reality show, it is very lightly scripted. We never know what the day might bring. Jerry Cohn and I have the habit of waking up early, long before dawn and an hour earlier than the other men. We try to find a big pot of coffee, and then we pray and seek the Lord and ask Him about His plans for the coming day. I always carry a leather-bound book with blank pages and as we pray, inspiration comes, and I start scribbling down the Holy Spirit Action Plan.

On your path, look for the practical way, but always be aware of the Holy Spirit guiding you. Remember that sometimes God asks you to do the impractical and even the seemingly impossible on your road of adventure, on your Proving Trail. So, as you pursue your goals, there will be changes; there will be detours; there will even be times when God says, "You have been aiming too low." So be prepared for God to adjust your path or maybe even your end goal. The plan is alive. It is fluid. It is a working plan in cooperation with God, not one set in stone.

Once you have decided on a course of action, whether it's big or small, *start*. Don't delay. Start—right now. God promises that He will give you "the want to." "For God is at work in you, both to will and to work for his good pleasure" (Phil. 2:13). When I pedaled my bicycle across the USA, how hard the first few miles were each day! But once I got rolling and the blood started pumping, I could pedal eighty more.

No matter where you find yourself right now, God is imminently present to you to empower you and guide you. Each morning, my bride and I ask Him to "open doors and close doors" as we open up our hearts to seek to do His will. Sometimes we look back at the week with a sense of wonder at what the tide of the Holy Spirit brought our way. Wonderful and wild things happen when we abide in His will. We are stoked to see God open unexpected doors and are even relieved when we see Him close doors that we hoped would open.

In both His "Yes!" and His "No," God is answering our prayers. We go when the light is green and come to a complete stop when the light is red. But there is also the yellow light that tells us to slow down and use caution as we proceed or pause. Or maybe the yellow light is God's saying "Yes—but not yet" or "Yes—but not with this person" or "Yes—but wait for my provision." And we are always attentive to the yield sign, always actively docile to God's will, like a good horse.

Even if it seems all Hell is breaking loose around you, stay the course. You will have a certain sense of peace, and there will be an inner joy in the midst of sorrow and supernatural strength in the midst of trial. For "the joy of the LORD is your strength" (Neh. 8:10). And it is "not by might, not by power, but my Spirit, says the LORD" (Zech. 4:6). When things seem impossible or too hard, that is when we get to see God work and experience His power and grace. That is where the adventure is.

So take courage, be wise, and move in God's timing when He beckons you. Just as a cowboy's powerful, trustworthy horse carries him along, let the power of the Holy Spirit carry you. Hang on and ride!

Step 6: *Discover the success and the happiness of pursuing your telos.* If we define *success* as moving in God's will, then the moment we take that first step in God's will each day, we are a success. If we are moving in virtue each day, we are fulfilling our nature, our calling, and our purpose. We are a success. Pursuing the goal *is* the goal.

There is a world of self-help books, of self-actualization primers, of instruction on how to pursue career success, but they miss the mark if they do not start off with the understanding that real success begins by knowing God and flowing in His purposes. Without this, life loses all meaning. "For whoever would save his life will lose it, but whoever loses his life for my sake will find it" (Matt 16:25). Instead of focusing so much on ourselves, focus on the Lord and on serving Him, and everything else will come into balance.

We learn from Dante that our life's purpose is not an inward, downward, self-centered spiral into Hell but an upward journey to Heaven. Beatrice showed Dante the Beatific Vision—a life of beatitude, a life questing to love God back, to be of service to Him, to be His friend, to do His will.

True success comes with true happiness. Ambition and accomplishment apart from God's purpose for your life is just emptiness.

There are two Scripture passages on success that really speak to me:

Joshua 1:8: "This book of the law shall not depart out of your mouth, but you shall meditate on it day and night, that you may be careful to do according to all that is written in it; for then you shall make your way prosperous, and then you shall have good success."

Psalm 1:1–3: "Blessed is the man ... [whose] delight is in the law of the LORD, and on his law he meditates day and night. He is like a tree planted by streams of water, that yields its fruit in its season, and its leaf will not wither. In all that he does, succeeds."

If your quest does not begin and end with a personal knowing of God, developed in prayer and reading the Bible—His love letter to you—if you do not have friendship with God, all that will come out of your pride is vainglory. Your earthly possessions will possess you. Jesus pointed to the way of Godliness as a path to happiness: "Seek first his kingdom and his righteousness, and all these things shall be yours as well" (Matt. 6:33).

It was Moses who entreated Joshua to walk in the ways of the Lord, promising that then—and only then—would he succeed. But Samuel, who came much later and anointed David as King, took those words of Moses about walking in the ways of the Lord. He told David that if you walk in the ways of the Lord, then you shall walk in the ways of the Lord. To walk along beside God is its own reward. God's friendship is the greatest possible reward.

The trail is the thing, not the
end of the trail. Travel too fast, and
you miss all you are traveling for.

—Louis L'Amour, *Ride thse Dark Trail*

Rule 8

Come Hell or High Water, Get the Job Done

*Every morning is a beginning, a fresh start, and a
man needn't be hog-tied to the past. Whatever went
before, a man's life can begin now, today."*

—Louis L'Amour, *Milo Talon*

Did you know that we have cowboys here in Hawaii? In fact, the
first hula that I learned was a dance about the Hawaiian Paniolos.
Back in 1793, when King Kamehameha was given five longhorns,
he hired Mexican cowboys to come and care for the herd. They
brought the same Cowboy Code to Hawaii that is lived today on the
mainland. Along with the Cowboy Way, they brought their small
guitars, which the Hawaiians reduced by two strings and retuned
and which in time came to be known as ukuleles. *Uke* means
"flea," and *lele* means "to dance." So *ukulele* means "dancing flea."

In turn, the Paniolos became familiar with the Hawaiian
ways and, in time, they became a part of our Hawaiian culture.
It was not hard for them to understand one of the key concepts
of the Hawaiian people—*kuleana*—because it is so consistent with
the Cowboy Code. *Kuleana* means having a sense of stewardship, even ownership of our responsibility. It is our dignity. We

identify our *kuleana* as being part of us—that we *malama pono*, "take good care of," something. And it is reciprocal: our *kuleana* also takes care of us.

This is the same reciprocal relationship that God intends for us with our work. Work is intended to be a blessing. Even before the Fall, God gave man *kuleana*. "The LORD God took the man," says Genesis, "and put him in the garden of Eden to till it and keep it" (Gen. 2:15). It is only because of man's fall that work has that element of toil.

Work was originally intended by God for our own good, and it still is. You see, God works—for example, in the work of creation, in His work of salvation, in His work in every person's life each day. Jesus said, "My Father is working still, and I am working" (John 5:17). If we are made in God's image, then we, too, are meant to work and, in fact, to find a certain fulfillment in it.

The garden of our *kuleana* must be built up, tended, and cared for. If no work is done, it either becomes overrun with weeds or it dies for lack of water and nutrients. Slothfulness destroys—and in this way, the slothful man is akin to the devil, who seeks only to "kill and steal and destroy" (John 10:10). In fact, sloth is considered one of the seven deadly sins, which put a man's soul in danger of Hell.

God prompts us, "Commit your work to the LORD, and your plans will be established" (Prov. 16:3)—"Every able man in whose mind the LORD had put ability, every one whose heart stirred him up to come to do the work" (see Exod. 36:2).

Cowboys love to write poetry. They love to philosophize as much as they love steak. Pope St. John Paul II served up the kind of red meat any cowboy would love when he issued, on September 14, 1981, the encyclical *Laborem Exercens* (Through

Work). Here is a piece of some good red meat—just a piece. I hope you have a knife and fork:

> Work is one of the characteristics that distinguish man from the rest of creatures, whose activity for sustaining their lives cannot be called work. Only man is capable of work, and only man works.... Man is the image of God partly through the mandate received from his Creator to subdue, to dominate, the earth. In carrying out this mandate, man, every human being, reflects the very action of the Creator of the universe.
>
> ... In spite of all this toil—perhaps, in a sense, because of it—work is a good thing for man. It is not only good in the sense that it is useful or something to enjoy; it is also good as being something worthy ... something that corresponds to man's dignity, that expresses this dignity and increases it.... He also achieves fulfillment as a human being and indeed, in a sense, becomes "more a human being."
>
> The Christian finds in human work a small part of the Cross of Christ and accepts it in the same spirit of redemption in which Christ accepted his Cross for us.

Work, from the beginning, was part of man's dignity in that God gave man dominion over the earth. Man was ordered to be fruitful and multiply and subdue the earth. Work was meant as a blessing.

God places such a high value on work that Scripture says, "A man is justified by works and not by faith alone" (James 2:24). It also says that "faith apart from works is dead" (James 2:26).

We perform the seven corporal works of mercy when we feed the hungry, give drink to the thirsty, clothe the naked, give shelter to travelers, visit the sick, visit the imprisoned, and bury the dead. We perform the seven spiritual works of mercy when we counsel the doubtful, instruct the ignorant, admonish the sinner, comfort the sorrowful, forgive injuries, bear wrongs patiently, and pray for the living and the dead.

But what about our day-to-day duties, chores, and jobs—such as a cowboy's mending a fence, cleaning the barn, or roping cows? Faith is at work when we exercise the virtues of justice, self-mastery, prudence, fortitude, faith, hope, and love in all the work that we do. That includes making our beds in the morning, doing the laundry, harvesting a field, selling life insurance, making coffee (although making coffee, in my estimation, is also a corporal work of mercy), welding, wiring a house, mopping floors, working in an office, or doing any form of productive work.

You and I have work to do—and not just today but on and on, even into our life in eternity. We get to work. Like Jesus, we will be about our "Father's work." No doubt there will be beautiful work for us to do in Heaven too, but it will be absent from the toil. Also, we won't be working out of fear of lacking food and shelter.

Perhaps you are now at what the world calls the "age of retirement." God has work for you too. In fact, these can be the most productive years of your life. You can serve in so many ways, especially in works of mercy. Even now, the "harvest is plentiful, but the laborers are few" (Matt. 9:37). God has a plan for you, to use you in His Kingdom right now, and it isn't to sit around watching the grass grow. Get off the couch, dude.

My wife, Cindy, is amazingly industrious. She always finds something productive to do in our home—things to clean, mend, make, paint, sew, or organize. She comes up with new recipes. She runs our household errands. If surprise visitors come by, before you know it, there is food and drink on the table. Her love graces our home with beauty.

It amazes me how Cindy always knows what present to give to someone. She always sees some need that she can fill in our friends' lives. She and I collaborate on my TV and radio shows and even on my books. Her active belief in me, and in our cause, sustains me when a third cup of coffee just won't do it. She is quick to point out when someone needs something from me or if there's someone whose life I can bless.

She does so many things that I may not even notice. She is always bettering our lives. She inspires me in my own work. But she also knows how to take time to play. Industriousness and hard work earn for us the time to play and to rest. Life must not just be about work. There must be play and enjoyment too. Right there in the word *recreation* is the word *re-create*. Play is a gift from God. It is the reward for hard work and a balanced life. I think that God finds as much pleasure when Cindy and I tandem-surf as when we travel to speak.

God wants us to be reliable, to get the job done. One of the weakest words in the English language is *try*. That word makes my blood boil. "Do or do not," as Master Yoda says. "There is no 'try.'" I have learned the hard way that you cannot rely on a man who, when you ask for his help, says, "I will try." As John Wayne was known to say, "Trying don't get the job done, son."

In the ninja dojo where I trained and taught, we resolved to never use the word *try*. That word is just a little escape hatch for the feeble will. We had a saying when doing our one hundred push-ups or unending sidekicks: "You can do one more of anything."

On the wall in one of the dojo classrooms were the words from King David: "Lead me to the rock too high to climb, and I will climb it" (see Ps. 61:2). David did not say "I will *try* to climb it." Jesus did not say, "I have come to *try* to do Your will, O God." No. He said, "I have come to do Your will" (see Heb. 10:7). There is no *try* in that verse or in the Lord. Rather, He "set his face like flint" (see Isa. 50:7; Luke 9:51) and headed up to Jerusalem to *do* the *work* of salvation until at last he could say: "It is finished" (John 19:30).

God wants workers with the grit and the determination to get the job done. He wants men to see something that needs doing and do it. He wants workers who take pride in their work, who do more than merely what is expected of them. He wants workers who take care of the small things, knowing that in doing so the big things take care of themselves.

God wants men with courage, fortitude, and integrity. He wants men with a mind to build something for themselves, for their country, and for their posterity. That means there are times when a man chooses between doing what he wants and doing what he must. Businesses and families are built by men doing what they ought to do.

I love the words of John Wayne in *Red River* when he challenges his men to join him on one of the longest cattle drives ever attempted: "Nobody has to come. There will still be a job for you when we get back. But remember this. Everyman who signs on for the drive agrees to finish it. There'll be no quitting along the way. Not by me. Not by you."

To a cowboy, being a quitter is as bad as being a horse thief. When someone quits, he leaves others holding the bag and having to do his work. Worse yet, he may be leaving them in serious danger. We need to carry our own backpacks.

A cowboy takes great pride in being a "top hand." What some might call hard work is, to a real ranch hand, just everyday chores. Cowboys work from can-see to can't, from sunup to sundown.

Pure and simple, they can be counted on to get the job done, come hell or high water. They live this verse: "Whatever your hand finds to do, do it with your might" (Eccles. 9:10). Ride for the brand. Be a top hand here on earth. Be His outstretched hand. Whatever work is set before you, do it.

Wouldn't you love to hear God say someday, "Well done, good and faithful servant" (Matt. 25:21)? When I was a boy, I worked alongside my dad on his many projects around the house. He taught me to be his right hand. He taught me not just to be there to help him but to anticipate the next tool he might need or the next thing that he might need me to do for him.

Later, when I started a new job, he taught me to write down a philosophy of work specific for that job. He told me that the first line of that philosophy should always be to help my boss to be successful and to meet his goals. If I felt that I could not be loyal to my boss in that way because he lacked integrity, then I should not go to work for him in the first place. In other words, I was to focus on the success of the whole business, not just my own. When I started my career, I had above my desk these words in a small frame that my mom gave me when I first started my career: "Do your work as unto the Lord and not as unto men, for it is from Him that comes your reward" (see Col. 3:23).

I met the same accusations. "Whoever is slack in his work is a brother to him who destroys" (Prov. 18:9).

God wants us to do a full day's work for a full day's pay. There is justice and dignity in this. In the movie *McLintock!*, a boy who was coming of age asked John Wayne's character to give him a job. Wayne's character responded, "Boy, you've got it all wrong. I don't give jobs. I hire men.... I will pay you a fair day's pay. I won't give you anything, and you won't give me anything. We both hold up our heads."

When I had my small CPA firm, I resolved not just to have good employees but only to have great employees. They knew this when they were hired on. I wanted to be able to trust them to be diligent in serving our clients. I set policies so that certain decisions had to be made only once, and we had procedures that were tight enough to ensure that work was done correctly and on time.

I trained my staff in a management style called "tight/loose." At first, I oversaw them very carefully; but once they had learned the ropes, I set them loose with just these words: "Okay. You got it now; it is all yours. But if you lose my confidence—if you start hearing me say the words 'Did you,' as in 'Did you get this done on time?' 'Did you follow our procedures?'—it will be time for you to move on."

Most of the staff rose to that standard. Only a few weeded themselves out. I provided my staff an environment where they could thrive, where they could grow in knowledge, skill, and ability, where they could take on all the new responsibilities and reap the financial blessings of their hard work. I helped several of them start their own businesses, and some went on to take over my practice when I moved to Hawaii.

My football coach used to exhort us, "When things get tough, the tough get going." When times are tough, you can run scared or reach back and grab the back of your saddle and lean in and ride. To say it bluntly, when it comes to work, be a man. Do all that is expected of you. Do more than is asked of you. My dad use to say, "If you're not ten minutes early for your job, you're late."

At the beginning of my twenty-five-hundred-mile bicycle ride across the United States, I had to cross mountains and deserts in record-breaking heat. As I looked into the distance, I could not tell whether I was seeing a mountain range or a mirage rising up from the ground in the heat of the day. It always seemed farther and farther away. I resolved to keep pedaling one stroke at a time, because I knew that, just as certain that I was riding into the desert, I was also on my way out the other side.

Running from responsibility is running from God's will. Running from God's will is running from God. That is a road to gradual deterioration and then sudden disaster.

When a man runs from his work, it only makes the work stack up on itself. It makes the man, and those he is called to serve, miserable. St. Paul wasn't messing around when he said, "If any one is not willing to work, let him not eat" (2 Thess. 3:10) and in another place, "If anyone does not provide for his relatives, and especially for members of his household, he has denied the faith and is worse than an unbeliever" (1 Tim. 5:8).

A cowboy must be resilient and reliable. To the extent possible in this world, a man needs to learn to be self-reliant. To the degree that a man relies on someone else to take care of things that he should do for himself, he loses his freedom. A man needs to saddle his own horse and rub it down and feed it at the end of the day.

A boy grows into a man when he accepts responsibility for himself and others. He either grows in this virtue or his soul atrophies, for "the soul of the sluggard craves and gets nothing, while the soul of the diligent is richly supplied" (Prov. 13:4).

As a Benedictine oblate, I seek to follow the *Rule of St. Benedict*. In his prologue, St. Benedict says this:

> The labor of obedience will bring you back to him from
> whom you have drifted through sloth and disobedience
> to do battle for the true King, Christ the Lord. First of
> all, every time you begin a good work, you must pray to

him most earnestly to bring it to perfection.... Clothed then with faith and the performance of good works, let us set out on this day ... that we may deserve to see him who has called us to His Kingdom.

You, as a man of God, have every reason for hope. When you come to an end of yourself you can win from there. Jesus even said to be cheerful about it: "In the world you will have tribulation. But be of good cheer. I have overcome the world" (John 16:33). Stay the course with the indomitable spirit and backbone that God gave you. Finish the job, come hell or high water.

We all experience those times when there seems no way out. As a surfer, sometimes, during a big wipeout and while enduring the long hold-down under water that comes with it, I just bring my arms in so that they don't get dislocated by the violence. I get in the fetal position. I don't fight the onslaught because I don't want to burn up my precious oxygen. I wait until it releases me and I get a sense of which way is up, and I swim to the light. Sometimes I hit bottom, and though it may be painful, at least I know which way is up and I can push off from there.

Hitting bottom isn't always a bad thing. It certainly helps a man get his bearings.

It can be that way, as you work your way back to God's will or through tough times. The more I am without oxygen, the more desperate it can feel. I may have pushed off from twenty feet below and I am only one foot from the surface, but the urgency I feel is greater as my lungs scream for air.

If you have hit bottom right now, good. That is a great place to start. You can push off from there. It is in those moments, if you lean in a bit and listen, you will hear God knocking on the door of your heart. And "if you hear His voice, do not harden your heart" (see Heb. 3:15).

No matter how many times you have stumbled or taken a dead-end detour, no matter how many times solid walls seem to rise up to block your path, God is still right there with you.

As we learned when we filmed *Long Ride Home*, the adventure truly does begin at the detour. Sometimes we mess up or are careless, and we find ourselves off-roading, away from the path that God intended for us. Sometimes the enemy may send us off on a tangent. At other times, life itself just careens into us and runs us into a ditch. Yet, no matter what, God is still right there with us. And He always uses the circumstances to our good. "For those who love God all things work together for good, for those who are called according to his purpose" (Rom. 8:28).

We have to get back in the saddle. God will lead us along a path of growth in virtue. The road is long and often painful, but strength comes through resistance training. Bearing this in mind, you can turn adversity into adventure. Move on in resolute determination. When we turn to God in those detours, He begins to work His will and His way into our hearts and into our lives. As soon as we repent and rethink the path we are on and say, "Your will be done," He starts moving in our hearts.

Our circumstances may not change right away, but *we* will change. We may have a long way to go to dig out from the hole we've dug for ourselves, but we can immediately be in His will in that we begin to seek the true good and enter into virtue in every small and big decision in our lives. I have heard someone ask, "How are you doing?" The response comes back: "Well, okay, under the circumstances." My question is: What are you doing under there? Rise up and obey Him in all things.

God uses these detours and the trials in our lives to shape us and tell His story through the adventure that He has for us. You are the clay, and He is the potter. You are the earthen vessel that the Master Craftsman is forming. As a man, you may be made out of mud, but you are called to be the earthen vessel of the Holy Spirit (see 2 Cor. 4:7). You are chosen to reveal a wonderful, adventurous story of God's love.

Ancient pottery often had a story etched into or painted on it. There is the story that God is etching and painting on the outside of this clay of your life. It is a story of defeat, of victory, of love, of sadness, of a bountiful harvest of great feats accomplished, of a life well lived!

Just as the potter presses water or oil into the clay and pounds it with his fist so that it becomes soft and pliable, so God pours the grace of His Spirit into your life and then uses the pressures and circumstance of your life to help you to become pliable and docile to His will. God intends for your life to be the story of His love and grace.

As He works with you and writes His story and perfects you, there comes a time for you to be tested by fire. Just as the potter puts his clay pot into the fiery furnace, so God proves you and tests you to establish you. Every clay vessel, before it is completed, is placed into a fiery furnace to establish it. The potter knows that it is not ready to come out of the fire until he can thump it with his finger and, instead of hearing a *thunk* of complaint and confusion, he hears that high, ringing sound of praise and thankfulness.

So please be patient with yourself. God is not finished with you yet. Just say yes to Him and praise Him in all things.

I love this verse, from the book of Sirach (which you won't find in a Protestant Bible):

My son, if you aspire to serve the Lord, prepare yourself for an ordeal ... for the chosen man is proven in the furnace of much affliction [the potter's furnace], but fall into the hands of God and not into the hands of man [do you see here the hands of the potter shaping and molding?], for what man has ever trusted in God and been left forsaken? For as great as his majesty is, so too is his mercy. (see Sir. 2:1, 5, 10, 18)

Yes, there will be testing in your life so that God can establish your trust in Him. But did you ever think that God has to trust in you too? God trusts that, during this time, you will not abandon Him, as some of His fickle fans did. "After this many of his disciples drew back and no longer went about with him. Jesus said to the twelve, 'Will you also go away?'" (John 6:66-67).

In this same way that fire tests and establishes the clay pot, so fire also purifies gold. The gold refiner places his ore in the cauldron and boils it. He continually scoops out the impurities and the dross until the gold is purified. He knows when the molten gold is purified because he can see his reflection in it. God similarly refines your faith, so "that the genuineness of your faith, more precious than gold which though perishable is tested by fire, may redound to praise and glory and honor at the revelation of Jesus Christ" (1 Pet. 1:7).

God's way is usually simple to figure out but not always easy to do. Satan is clever and brings confusion, but the Holy Spirit brings order out of chaos.

It is the willingness to accept responsibility,
I think, that is the measure of a man.

—Louis L'Amour, *Bendigo Shafter*

Rule 9

Lean and Mean: Fitness to Witness

Whoever heard of a revolution of fat men?
—Louis L'Amour, *To the Far Blue Mountains*

The Wild West was a tough country. If you had not toughened up your body with sinew and muscle, you probably would not have lasted long there. Even today, a cowboy has to work as hard as an athlete. He has to be lean in the saddle and have a grip like a vice, the strength to deal with an ornery bull, and the stamina to work a full, long day and perhaps a night—from can-see to can't.

The early monks were tough too. They defined their discipline in life and worship by using the Greek word *askesis*, which was used to describe Olympic athletes in "training." It's where we get the word *ascetic*. The monks considered themselves God's athletes.

Mind you, athletes in those days competed not only in track and field and wrestling but also in deadly combative sports. If they wanted the victor's crown, they had to fight for it.

And so it was that the early monks embraced an ascetic life in eating, drinking, work, and prayer. They, too, meant to stay the course. They lived a spiritual martyrdom as they surrendered everything to God to "fight the good fight." They were tough men, both physically and spiritually.

In my second year of college, I saw a couple of the young men I had played football with in high school and noticed they had really let themselves go. I decided then and there that I would remain an athlete my whole life.

What about men today? How good a job are we doing as stewards of our bodies, God's temples? Do we have the fitness to fulfill the mission God has given us? Does our fitness attest to our witness of being men of God? Do our bodies express God's handiwork? Does our fitness affirm that we live lives of manly virtue, or do our bodies point to two mortal sins: sloth and gluttony?

Within the word *discipline* is the word *disciple*. Does our physical fitness express that disciplined ascetic of those ancient athletes for Christ with a quality of restraint in eating and a willingness to work out and to do the things that it takes to remain strong and fit?

I'm just going to say it as it is. The contrast between the athletic lifestyle of most Hawaiians versus the visitors to the islands is not just shocking: it is alarming. Hawaii is considered the fittest state in the nation. Most people who live in Hawaii are fit not because they go to a gym but because they play and have an active lifestyle and moderate what they eat. What is especially alarming to me is how many of the young men who visit here are so caught up in computer games that their necks have developed a kind of stoop from leaning over on their keyboard and looking at their monitors. They play a sports game on their computer rather than going outside and *playing the sport*!

In Hawaii, we see dads and moms out with their sons and daughters doing something athletic; or we see children out on the beach or in the ocean or at the park playing all day.

The obesity rate in men in the United States over the last three decades has tripled. In 1990, it was 12 percent; now it is over 40 percent. By the way, there is a reason why you do not see a lot of older obese people. They died young. Overall physical wellness has declined. The life expectancy of a man drops every year. The obesity rate in women is even more alarming. What are you men going to do about your own fitness so that you can lead your family by example?

Or are you going to die young and not live to see your children's children? Even if you do live a long time, will you be too unfit to enjoy your family and your life and fulfill God's calling for you? In time, because of your own laxness, you will become a burden to your family. It happens sooner than you think.

Has your body become more fat than muscle? Are you attractive to your wife? Are you physically fit enough to genuinely please her?

Do you have the stamina and the strength to put in a hard day's work and then come home and love on your family, or coach little league, or even play ball in the yard? How about having the energy to really listen to your wife and children as they tell you about their day? Or to play with your children instead of nodding off in your easy chair because you are out of shape?

When is the last time you set a physical challenge for yourself?

Is your resting heart rate higher than room temperature or down in the fifties, where it belongs? Do you even *know* your resting heart rate? You should. How about your endurance? If you had to, how far could you run, walk, or swim? If you had to fight someone to protect your family, how long could you last?

Look at it this way: if you knew Jesus was stopping by for a cup of coffee tomorrow afternoon, wouldn't you spend all day organizing and cleaning to prepare for Him? What if you knew that God was coming to make His home in your body? Well, He has already done that. Your body is the temple of the Holy Spirit. As the keeper of the Lord's home, how well do you take care of your body? Is the Lord pleased with how you are maintaining His dwelling place?

How often do you exercise? Do you eat according to a regimen that avoids bad food and provides you with the fuel and the nourishment that you need and your body deserves? Do you take supplements? What about your flexibility training, your hydration, and your sleep? How strong is your grip? How much can you lift? What is your muscular strength? Science is discovering that the number-one thing that helps mental acuity is resistance and cardio training.

God has a plan for your life. Do you have the stamina, the strength, and the overall health to rise to the challenge of that call?

The very fact that you are reading this book says that you already have the intent to live a life of manly virtue.

Did you know that you can train in all seven virtues from the outside in? You can train in self-mastery (temperance), fortitude, prudence, justice, faith, hope, and love all while training your body, giving your body what it so badly wants and needs. I am not saying that you need to become a gym rat. I am not saying to focus on your body so much that it becomes a god to you. But I *am* challenging you to place value on your body and take care of it, as you would any piece of equipment in your garage.

We are not souls living in bodies. Our bodies and souls are one, and yet we sometimes neglect our bodies as if they are just shells for our souls.

Every year, I set a fitness challenge for myself. Over the years, it may have been to obtain a new martial-art belt level, compete in a world title for tandem surfing, pedal my bicycle across the United States, or paddle my tandem surfboard across the treacherous thirty-five-mile channel between the islands of Molokai and O'ahu. All of these fitness efforts were more an act of virtue than a physical act. I learned that challenging myself with fitness goals like this required me to grow in the virtues of fortitude, self-mastery, and prudence—in fact, in all of the virtues.

When you excel in fitness, it tends to spill over into excelling in all areas of your life; plus, it is your way of showing your appreciation to God for the miraculous body He gave to you. It is an act of justice toward God to care for the body He gave to you, and, in turn, God rewards you, as you grow in fitness, with the release of natural "feel good" endorphins. A man's physical fitness shouts pretty loudly about his virtue. What does your fitness level say about your virtue?

One of the first things a lot of men do when they join Bear's Man Cave[6] is to take a personal inventory, and one of those areas is physical fitness. Most men lose a substantial amount of weight when they first join us. Many of our men have lost more than twenty pounds. Some shed more than one hundred pounds as part of their pursuit of manly virtue and obedience to God.

But why should you listen to me about health and fitness? Good question. Let me tell you.

As you know, I have been an athlete all my life. I have excelled in martial arts, having earned two black belts as well as teaching credentials in several other fighting forms. I participate in many ocean waterman sports, and I compete in various surfing events around the world. In fact, I have won two Masters World

---

[6] See Bear Woznick's Deep Adventure Ministries, www.bearschool ofmanliness.com.

Tandem Surfing titles past the age of fifty-five. I have coached world champions and taught many competitive teams. About half of the lineage of those who compete in the sport today can find their way back to me, as my students have become teachers in their own right.

Tandem surfing is physically demanding, as it involves lifting a woman in one of more than fifty extreme overhead lifts while carving on a wave. I still tandem-surf and lift my wife today. In fact, we fell in love on a tandem surfboard. To compete in this sport, the woman has to weigh at least half as much as the man. So, if I gain weight, my partner has to do so as well, which obviously is not an option. There is no place to run and hide your weight at the public weigh-in that takes place before every event, so I have had to learn the key to maintaining my "fighting weight."

I think I have earned the right to offer you my thoughts in this area for you to at least consider.

My DNA consists of two different lines of Viking blood, so I can gain muscle easily but I can just as easily gain fat. I am half Norwegian; the other half is Ukrainian, and the Ukraine was settled by Vikings. I have learned how to build and maintain muscle mass while losing fat and keeping it off.

Consider what has worked for me and what has worked and not worked for you, and do your own homework and then set measurable goals in each area.

The way I stay fit is to make it fun and to make it a game. Instead of training, I am playing. I will admit, however, when training for a black belt or a world surfing title, that it feels more like going to war. But, as my tandem-surfing lifting coach and world-champ stunt cheerleader Kelvin Lam told me, after a particularly grueling workout of crabwalks in the sand and then running in the sand with my tandem partner standing on my shoulders: "It's hard work, isn't it? But you know what is really fun? Winning."

Part of making fitness fun is having a partner in crime to pursue it with. Cindy and I have a great time working out, surfing, snorkeling, sailing, hiking, and golfing, among so many other things. We also are on the same low-sugar-carb eating regimen.

Sometimes we walk down to Dukes on Sunday and dance for a half hour on the beach. In the morning, we walk to get hot coffee, pray, and then take a quick swim. After lunch and dinner, we usually go for a surf or a beach walk and another short swim. I do my flexibility stretching on my Pilates machine before dinner while I watch a fun show. Do you see? It's a game. Our fitness regimen is something that often brings Cindy and me together as a couple. They're like mini-dates. It's fun. God makes it even more fun by pumping out the feel-good endorphin hormone as a reward for giving our bodies the workouts they want.

When I was about thirty and worked for a big corporation, my coworkers and I all took a morning, lunch, and afternoon break together, sitting in the employee dining room. In other words, my job was to sit all day. One day, I heard that still, small voice of God inside my heart say as clear as a bell: "You are my walking man. Now go walk." I started walking and praying at every break. When I started my own CPA practice, I began to hike in the Southern California mountains at lunch. At night, after my children went to bed, I hiked under the stars.

When I moved to Hawaii in the late nineties, I decided to make my walks into a game. I bought a Garmin GPS watch so I could get in at least fifty miles of beach walking and surfing each week. Now fitness scorekeeping is even more fun. I use my Fitbit to be sure I get at least seven and a half hours of actual sleep each night, that I burn 3,575 calories each day, and that I get in my 11,500 steps or paddle strokes. My Fitbit is telling me right now that yesterday I burned 3,656 calories, but the day before I burned only 2,998. So I have some catching up to do to reach my 25,000-per-week calorie-burn goal. Fitness should be fun. It should be a game. But in order for it to be a game, you need to keep score.

Even eating is a game to me. I do not count calories. I just count sugar carbs. My goal is twenty-five grams or less per day.

For some people, the most fun part of their day is playing racquetball or pickleball or tennis, or biking or hitting the weight rack or flexibility training or CrossFit training, or swimming or running or walking or golfing. Even cleaning the house or washing your car can be a good burn.

Having a partner in crime—a training partner—helps. At one point, I had a group text with three friends of mine. As the day went on, each of us, in turn, would text "60/60/60/60." That text just meant that the person posting had done sixty push-ups, sixty crunches, sixty minutes of cardio, and sixty minutes of prayer and reading. Of course, some prayer and reading can be done while doing cardio. Also, push-ups and crunches are a cardio workout, so that kills two birds with one stone. The time commitment to do this was more like ninety minutes, not four hours. The point is that we challenged and inspired each other.

Right now, my good friend Pat Gervais and I have a contest. We weigh in once a week, and whoever loses more weight wins. The loser has to go out in public and record a video of himself singing out loud the song for that week. This week, Pat has to sing "What Is Love?" the way Will Ferrell sang it in *A Night at the Roxbury*, head bob included. I am motivated by fear because I don't want to sing and humiliate myself in public; I am even more motivated by the anticipation of seeing Pat belt out his song.

Being fit also prepares you to have the best chance of recovery from an illness or injury. When I speak to groups of athletes, I ask for anyone who does not have an injury at the moment to raise his hand. Very few raise their hands. Athletes are always rehabbing an injury and working around that injury to maintain their fitness. Injury should usually not be an excuse. There is usually some sort of fitness training you can do, and if you do it, your recovery will go better.

When I was training to compete in my first World Tandem Surfing Championship down under in Australia, I was also doing a six-month test for my first black belt. During the training, I ended up tearing a meniscus. After surgery, the only cardio that I could do was sit-ups. So I did one thousand per day. There is almost always a work-around of some sort for an injury so you can maintain some fitness.

When injury or illness comes, it can really cut you down physically. You want to stay in shape so that, as the injury or illness takes its toll, you are starting from a good place. In the last three years, I have had to have surgery to reattach my bicep muscle, which was torn loose while I dropped into a big wave. I also had to have part of my hip muscle reattached after it was torn loose when I flipped my outrigger canoe while surfing it down the face of a hollow wave.

When I could not walk distances during my rehab, I did Pilates workouts and light swims. In the last few years, I have even had to fight to come back from radiation treatment for prostate cancer. I just keep going back to my fitness regimen.

This regimen has served me well while I compete in surfing. It has served me well during illness and injury. It has served me well during times of complete health. Cindy has lived on a very similar regimen for most of her adult life. Please consider the following aspects of a fitness regimen and take the things that you think will work for you and add them to your toolbox.

Eating Regimen

Back in the nineties, when I was training to compete in my first world title, an athlete's eating regimen had become very confusing. We were told untruths: "Stop the insanity! Fat makes you fat!" The new "food pyramid" developed by the grain industry had turned the traditional eating pattern upside down, making grains and fruit (the two primary sources of sugar carbs, also known as "God's candy") the primary food groups. We were told to avoid red meat and fat at all costs.

I trained hard before my first World Tandem Surfing competition to gain muscle while trying to drop my weight. I ate bagels for breakfast (because there was no butter or fat in them) and drank fruit smoothies. I realize now that I was defeating myself. These were full of sugar carbs. Basically, I was throwing gasoline on the fire of my hunger. I felt as if there was a furnace raging in me that needed more food, and it took tremendous discipline to stay on my "athlete's diet." I stayed away from eggs, bacon, and red meat. In other words, in order to drop weight, I had fallen into the trap of staying away from protein and good fat. To make matters worse, as I slowly lost body fat, I realized that I was losing a lot of muscle too.

Just before I was supposed to fly to Australia for the world title, I had a chance to escape to Catalina Island and stay at Zane Grey's Pueblo. My plan was to do my last round of training to cut weight before the contest. Something happened there that forever changed my life. On the morning that I was to catch the ferry to go back to the mainland, I went out for my usual breakfast of a bagel and a fruit smoothie. I looked over at the table next to me and saw about a dozen very athletic, strong, and fit people enjoying a big breakfast of steak, eggs, cheese omelets, bacon, and sausage.

I just had to ask them. "How do you stay so fit when you eat like that?" They looked at me as if I was going to be their newest recruit and said, "Dude, don't laugh. It is that old diet our moms were on. It's the Atkins diet. We live the Atkins way."

"Yeah, I remember that," I said. "It really worked for my mom and her friends. What is that all about anyway?"

They said, "It's simple. The best thing is that you get to eat all the food you want so long as you keep your sugar carbs between seventeen and twenty-five grams a day. But here's the good news: when you stop taking in so many sugar carbs, you are no longer hungry all the time. Plus, protein is a natural diuretic, so you lose about three pounds of inflammation and water within the first four or five days of your new lifestyle."

Another person chimed in: "In fact, you forget to eat. Your body is no longer in open rebellion against you. And then, when you do get hungry, it seems to come from an entirely different place. It's like your body is just saying, 'Feed me. I need fuel.'"

I started my new life right then and there and never looked back. I pushed away the bagel and juice and ordered a cheese omelet with a side of bacon. I went to the bookstore the next day and bought an Atkins book and learned that I could eat all the fiber, carbs, protein, and good fat that I wanted. I just had to keep my sugar carbs below twenty grams a day.

In no time, I was dropping weight and gaining muscle mass. It seemed that I had limitless energy, I had no sugar-carb coma after eating, and I slept deeply and soundly. I learned which alcoholic drinks were the lowest in sugar, and I actually learned to avoid alcohol completely when peaking for a contest because it restricts protein synthesis.

Every elite athlete has his own eating regimen, but most athletes live an Atkins lifestyle or what we now refer to as a Keto regimen. Cindy began to live a low-sugar-carb regimen back in the nineties, about the same time that I did, long before we met—and trust me, she is ripped.

Do you ever find yourself saying that you are hungry all the time and wonder if there is something medically wrong with you? You can fix that in just three days when you switch to a Keto regimen.

Vitamins and Mineral Supplements

I also have been taking vitamins and mineral supplements my whole life. The last thing my mom gave to me when I headed off to college was a big bottle of daily vitamins. When I was forty-eight years old, I paddled the treacherous thirty-five-mile Kaiwi Channel between the islands of Molokai and O'ahu. It took me ten hours and nineteen minutes, and I had a total of only six minutes of rest. The next morning, I had breakfast with legendary big-wave rider and waterman Ken Bradshaw, who is about my age. After breakfast, I reached into my pocket and took out a small bag of supplements; at the very same moment, he did the same. We both realized that one of the reasons we could both still excel athletically at our age was the benefits of our supplements.

After I won my first world title, I was sponsored by Joe Rogan's Onnit supplement company and have found those supplements to be the very best. I am considered now one of their OGs. You can buy them at our deepadventure.com store website. I recommend that you do your research and find a supplement regimen that works for you and stick to it.

Hydration and Electrolytes

I know this sounds weird, but I do not like to drink plain water, so I drink some form of sparkling water mixed with regular water. After my morning cups of coffee, I switch to drinking this throughout the day. If you do not get those eight glasses of water in a day, you will find that your body freaks out and you start retaining water, that you are hungry, and that you have trouble sleeping. Drinking the proper amount of water also helps you to develop muscle tissue and helps your muscles recover from physical activity. Be sure to drink electrolytes to keep your chemicals in balance during strenuous workouts.

Strength Training

It is important to set appointments with yourself for your fitness training and to establish a rhythm. All-Pro Kansas City Chiefs running back Christian "the Nigerian Nightmare" Okoye taught me something about this when I taught him how to surf. Even though he had retired from football, he was still ripped and fit. When I asked him how he stayed in such great shape, he just said, "It is simple. Every morning at six a.m., I have an appointment with myself. Everyone knows that I have this appointment, and they don't dare schedule anything with me first thing in the morning." Set a training regimen. Make a daily fitness appointment with yourself.

During my early world title chases, I hit the gym just about daily, doing deadlifts, bench presses, leg lifts, curls for the girls, and intense ab workouts. I loved going to the gym. It was a blast, especially when I trained with workout partners, such as Jeff Owens and future world champ tandem surfer Chuck Inman. Having an appointment with them helped me to keep the appointment that I had with myself.

That is the key: have a regular standing appointment with yourself and perhaps with a training partner. Have a fitness schedule, and track your metrics. Keeping score makes it a game.

I no longer hit the weights like I used to. I have since switched my strength and resistance training to stand-up paddle (SUP) surfing. It is more fun and more effective. Gym weights can make you strong, but they build muscle in a rigid way that can inhibit your muscle from being effective in natural, flowing, athletic endeavors. CrossFit training or P90X workouts are designed to overcome this. I have really benefited from those systems in the past, but now, for me, I have found that SUP surfing is the best overall fitness regimen I have ever had. It builds core strength and leg and arm strength. It probably even makes your eyelids stronger! I have a friend whose fallen arches were fixed after one year of regular SUP surfing. It hits every muscle group—and in a way that makes those muscles functional. Find a strength-training regimen and vary it so that it is fun; that way, you will more likely stick with it, and the muscle confusion will build on muscle strength.

Cardio and Endurance Training

Even though I was a running back, I never liked to run. My coaches were shocked to see how slowly I lumbered along when they timed us. When Chuck Inman and I worked out together, we started out with a warm-up of running up the twenty-five flights of stairs to my condo. He would give me a much-needed head start and then try to catch up with me.

Finally, one day, I said, "Chuck, I am getting in good shape. I think I can give you a run for your money. You take off, and when you reach the second floor, yell. I will try to catch you." He took off, and, when he yelled, I quickly dashed out of the stairwell and took the elevator to the twenty-third floor. I listened next to the stairwell door, and when I heard him trudge past me, beleaguered, I quietly opened the door and sprinted up to pass him.

I exuberantly thanked him for all of his effort in being my trainer and how it had really paid off. "In fact," I said, "I feel so great. Let's do it again!" I savored those two victories, reminding him of it regularly, until finally I just could not stand it anymore and broke down and told him what I had done. Needless to say, he did not find it as hysterically funny as I did.

In the past, I have gotten in my cardio training by mountain biking, hiking, and walking on the beach, but now I get my cardio by SUP surfing. When I SUP surf, my heart rate stays above 150. When I am paddling hard to catch a wave or stay in it, as I am paddling back out up and over waves, or as I paddle the mile back to my condo into the trade winds, my heart rate stays high. Whether you get your cardio on a stationary bike, by playing racquetball or pickleball, or by swimming, the point is to set a daily goal and do it. Make it a game.

My endurance and cardio daily goal is one hour with my heart rate above 120: SUP surfing, spear fishing, and walking the beach; to some degree, walking the golf course does this for me too because I am such a bad golfer. I have so much fun golfing—but it is not so much fun for the people on the adjacent fairway!

Flexibility Training

I had UFC champ Bas Rutten on *The Bear Woznick Adventure* radio show and podcast once, and I asked him about his flexibility training. He told me that he goes out to his backyard every day and does his flexibility training while he prays his morning Rosary.

Cindy does flexibility training at least four times a week. I used the P90X workouts, which include flexibility training, leading up to my world title chase; I focused on Pilates. I trained seven hours a week just on flexibility. Now I spend about twenty minutes a day on it. Flexibility is essential to performance, but even more important, it helps prevent muscle strains and injuries that can occur in just our everyday routines.

Cindy and I have a Pilates Reformer in our home. It was designed by Joseph Pilates, who used to train dancers in the theater district in New York. It works tremendously for my flexibility, but it's also excellent for strength and cardio. It's a great longevity tool too. Pilates was instrumental in my winning my two tandem-surfing world titles.

Men have asked me, "I know I need to get in better shape, but where do I get the motivation?" Just look at your wife and your children. Do you want to stay actively involved in their lives? Do you want to take care of them—or do you want them to end up caring for you?

It is true in every area of your life, but it is more obvious in your physical fitness. You are either getting stronger or weaker. God has a mission for you. Be fit for the challenge.

> For you and me, today is all we have;
> tomorrow is a mirage that
> may never become reality.

—Louis L'Amour, *The Walking Drum*

Rule 10

Build Brotherhood

Up to a point a man's life is shaped by environment, heredity,
and movements and changes in the world about him; then
there comes a time when it lies within his grasp to shape
the clay of his life into the sort of thing he wishes to be.

—Louis L'Amour, *The Walking Drum*

I rode my truck down the narrow, dusty dirt road that runs parallel to the North Fork Flathead River, which serves as the western boundary into Glacier National Park in Montana. I drove across a short bridge over the cold, clear, rushing waters of Trail Creek, just two miles south of the Canadian border, and turned onto the entrance to the eight acres of raw timbered land that I had recently scraped together enough money to buy.

It was an entrance; that was all. There was no real road to access the low ridgeline a short way to my property. At least, I thought it was my property. I grabbed my shotgun, loaded with two slugs, and started to walk into my land to the site where I would build, with my own hands and the help of my children, a small hunter's cabin.

As I walked in along a clearing, I saw the real owner of the land seeing me. A lone gray wolf, which must have weighed close to 150 pounds, glared at me, piercing me with his fluorescent yellow eyes as if to say, "What the hell are you doing on my land?" Wolves are apex predators. They are big and mean, and they know it. He watched me menacingly as I continued on.

Our uneasy relationship went on like that for several months. I would see him from time to time as I worked on preparing the land for my cabin or as I walked along the ridgeline to the Flathead River. There is a certain berry on that ridgeline that the grizzlies love to feast on, and it was an everyday thing to see fresh signs of a bear, a wolf, or a mountain lion. It gave a man a wary feeling when the call of nature came in the morning, and I never knew what might be sneaking up behind the stump that I happened to be using. I guarantee you that the outhouse went up as soon as the cabin was built enough to be closed in.

From time to time, I would hear the engine of a low-flying Cessna 172 as the pilot circled above, trying to hone in on radio signals from mountain lions, bears, and wolves that scientists had tagged for tracking. When those planes got close enough for me to see—or, worse yet, began to circle an area near me—I knew that a tagged predator was near me, and I moved on in the opposite direction. I was in no hurry to be on someone's lunch menu.

That lone wolf looked menacing, but he also looked a bit gaunt, which seemed strange to me because the forest was thick with game for him to hunt. I found out why a few months later, when I came to meet one of those trackers who flew those planes.

It was late October, after the leaves had fallen, after the migrating birds had gone and animals were holing up for hibernation, and the first snows had blanketed the ground with a few inches of snow that hushed the sound of the forest. No breeze blew, and no sound was heard—not an insect buzzing, a bird chirping, or even a leaf falling. I never knew a quietness like this. When you leave the city, you come to realize how loud nature can be. But not today.

As I sat that afternoon on my porch in solitude and stillness, with only the rhythmic sound of my heart and breath in my ears, I thought I heard a voice.

It's hard to explain this, but when it is that quiet, even an imagined sound in your mind can seem real. When it is this quiet, a man can seem to hear a sound that is only in his mind.

I held my breath for a moment and stilled my body so that not even the sound of my sleeve in motion could be heard. Then I caught the sound again. Something big was moving my way. Was it a big buck or a bull elk coming down from the high country? Whatever it was, it was definitely approaching my cabin porch. My skin crawled as I wondered if it was a predator. Then I heard it: "Hello, the cabin!" shouted a man's voice. I stood up, shotgun in hand, and waved him in. I told him he was the first person I had seen in this area in a long time.

He had a ready smile and a demeanor that put me at ease. He told me that he was one of those pilots I had seen flying overhead. He was a professor at the University of Montana in Missoula. He said that he was on foot tracking a lone wolf. The bear claw tied with some sort of animal hide around the brim of his cowboy hat told me he was the real deal.

I mentioned the lone wolf that I had been seeing from time to time, and he figured that it was probably the lone wolf he was tracking. I asked him about that wolf and why it chose to run alone instead of in a pack, and he told me its story. "You see," he said, "wolves run in packs. They hunt in packs. They chase down, corner, and then surround their prey and then go in for the kill. They like fresh meat, so they bring down an animal regularly. It might be a yearling deer or young elk, or one that is weak or somehow got separated from the rest of his herd."

"But," he went on to say, "a lone wolf is a special case of anger and hunger. He's a former alpha male, the leader of the pack, that lost his role and was forced out of the pack by a younger, tougher wolf. Lone wolves do not last long because it is hard for them to hunt alone. He will eventually grow weak from hunger. Disease will catch up with him. He'll drop dead or be picked off by another apex predator. His normal life expectancy is much shorter than that of the rest of the wolves that run together in the pack."

Ponder that for a moment. Men today take pride in saying that they are a "lone wolf." They isolate themselves. They have no true friendships with other men. When they are together with other men, they hide themselves in their own failings and fears. They insulate themselves from other men with small talk about sports or politics or their latest victory over crabgrass.

These "lone wolves" never really open up and truly walk alongside other men. They don't want to admit that they've got something gnawing at their guts. They don't want to show any weakness or vulnerability. But it is all a facade. Someday—hopefully, before they crack or just fade out—they will find out that other men are just like them. We are all bozos on the same bus, trying our best to work things out.

That's why men need friends. We need brothers. We need a pack. It's easy for a man to come home after a long day's work and just slide into a pattern of turning on the news, watching sports, gaming, or, worst of all, sneaking into a pattern of viewing pornography.

On the other hand, perhaps they are seeking to go deeper with God, so they read and they study and they pray. But without

fellowship with other men, they have difficulty getting deep traction in manly virtue because there are no other men who will
stand with them when times get tough or come along beside
them and inspire them to heroic manliness.

Men are not intended to be lone wolves or lone rangers. We
are meant to be a pack. We are meant to be a brotherhood. Lone
wolves are easy prey. They are like spiritual toddlers meandering
aimlessly through the streets during a war with bullets flying all
around them.

The fate of the men who isolate themselves from other men
is like that of a lone wolf. They will have the tendency to grow
weaker or unbalanced. They never grow into full manliness. In
their isolation, they grow gaunt spiritually and morally. They're
easy prey for the enemy. His weakness and vulnerability have
consequences that are devastating to him, his family, and those
he has responsibility for.

In the days of Moses, as God led the nomadic children of
Israel in the wilderness, the Amalekites would strike at those
who straggled behind or who wandered off a bit—in other words,
those who were isolated and alone and were easy pickings.

This enemy was always a thorn in the side of Israel. Amalek
was the grandson of Esau. You remember him. He was the hunter
who gave up his inheritance, as a firstborn son, to his younger
brother, Jacob (who came to be called Israel), in exchange for a
bowl of soup.

Since that day, Esau's descendants, the Edomites and the
Amalekites, were a plague to the children of his brother, Israel,
from Moses until the time of Jesus. King Saul was told to destroy
every one of them. But when he captured them, he did not destroy them. He paid for this transgression by losing his kingship,
and the Amalekites continued attacking Israel for generations.

While David and his men were out fighting, the Amalekites descended on the town of Ziklag. They plundered it and took all the residents captive. David arrived just after the attack and, without hesitating, took off in hot pursuit. He managed to re-cover the women and children and all the plunder that had been taken. He also killed all the Amalekites, except for four hundred who escaped on camels.

The Persian king Xerxes had a prime minister named Haman, a descendant of Agag, the king of the Amalekites. Haman tricked the king into ordering an edict to kill all of the Hebrew nation who had been captured and taken there as exiles. The king did not know that his own queen, Esther, was a Jewess. When she revealed all this to the king, he issued another edict, allowing the Hebrews to defend themselves. And so they did. Haman had built ten gallows for the Jews to be hanged on, but, in the end, it was he and his ten sons who were hanged there.

King Herod was a descendant of Esau too. We know how he wickedly and cowardly committed infanticide, killing all the male children two years old and younger in Bethlehem in an attempt to assassinate the newborn King of Israel. It was a son of Herod, who had his same name, who sat at Christ's trial.

To this day, the demon spirit of Amalek, the son of the hunter Esau, is still hunting the stragglers, those who isolate themselves, who are easy pickings.

Moses defeated that ancient enemy and shows us today how to do the same. There was a great battle being fought between the Hebrew nation and the Amalekites at a place called Rephidim. The men of Israel joined together and supported one another as brothers and won the battle.

As the battle raged below the mountain where Moses stood with two of his men, he raised his arms to God. As long as he held his arms up, Israel had the advantage. But as he grew tired and lowered his arms, the tide turned against Israel. So they placed a big rock under Moses so he could sit down. Is this not, of course, the rock of Christ, whom we trust in all our battles?

As the fight raged on and Moses grew wearier, he had no choice but to lower his arms from time to time. But then something happened that must be a lesson for all men today. Two men—Aaron, Moses' brother, and Hur—stood on either side of Moses and supported his arms. Israel went on to win a great victory that day.

The name of that battle ground, *Rephidim*, means "support." Every man today is in a battle. Amalek is on the hunt for you. You are in a fight to the death with an enemy who wants to isolate you and destroy you. How do you win that fight? First, you must trust in Jesus the Rock. Second, you must have the support of trusted brothers who will stand beside you in the fight and whom you, in turn, will support.

To thrive, to be fully alive, to be activated and have his potential fully actualized, a man must be consistently in the company of other good men. That's the pattern that Jesus instituted with His twelve disciples, whom He called friends. Be alert to the men that God has brought into your life and seek to build brotherhood with them. If you do not find true brothers there, you must search them out in a men's group.

I also warn you to be wary of those who can do you no good at all and to stay away from them. Don't hang out with the wrong crowd. "Blessed is the man who walks not in the counsel of the wicked, nor stands in the way of sinners, nor sits in the seat of scoffers" (Ps. 1:1).

In the ancient world, it was the habit of men to hang around by the city gates. They would check out who was coming in and out of town and gather the latest news. In Hawaii, we call it "talking story." Who do you hang around with? Do you hang around with strong men, good men perhaps, men who are better than you are at the moment or who are more accomplished in areas that you aspire to grow in—men who can inspire you to grow in manly virtue? Or are the men you hang out with just getting by, just passing through life, just nice guys—or, worse, men who are defeated, going nowhere fast, with no moral compass, no purpose, no cause to champion? They reach for a beer instead of for the stars. Here is a question to ask yourself: How do they speak of and treat women?

My friend and champion surfer Girard Middleton was the chaplain of the University of Miami national championship baseball and football teams. He saw the commitment of these young men, both to individual excellence and to one another. The pursuit of their common goal forged strong bonds of brotherhood.

Soon, Girard began to measure his own relationships by these bonds of brotherhood. He says it this way. Should this person be on my championship diet? Is he healthy for me? "Is this someone who will challenge me along a path of righteousness and excellence, or will he drag me down?"

The best way to stay out of trouble is to stay away from it in the first place. Some people *are* trouble and are of no good to you with their foul language, the way they speak about women, and their disrespect for the true good. Don't give them a place in your life.

In the Sacrament of Reconciliation, Catholic men pledge to God to avoid the "near occasion of sin." Among other things, this means to avoid certain people. Do you want to lead these man-boys to Christ? Then separate from them and show them how a man of virtue lives. Stand apart from them so you can

stand tall, and then perhaps you can raise them up. But don't
let them drag you down to their level.

You should also avoid men who do not keep their word to
you, who do not shoot straight, and who mislead you and who
betray you. They are opportunists, who appear to be your friend
only so that they can get something from you. Be wary. If it smells
like a rat, it probably is a rat. Forgive them and move on, or
perhaps you can give a man a second chance, but be wary. There
is no virtue in trusting easily. This is counter to the virtue of
prudence. Trust must be earned, but we must be open to giving
people a chance to earn it. When we find someone we trust, we
must treasure that person as one of the great riches in our lives.
Even Jesus has this test: if "you have been faithful over a little,
I will set you over much" (see Matt. 25:21).

Now that I have given this "surgeon general's warning," I do
encourage you to pursue manly friendships. Find a men's group,
or perhaps even start one. It only takes three men to do so. Value
the men in your life. Build up and strengthen the friendships
you have and be grateful for them. Just like that car in the garage
that needs regular maintenance, so do your friendships. Do not
take them for granted.

Brotherhood is most deeply forged when men face adversity
together. Working in a Christmas tree lot together in the cold
of winter may forge some of the strongest bonds among the
Knights of Columbus. True fellowship is developed when fel-
lows are all in the same ship, rowing together, pulling together
toward a common goal.

How about doing something really bodacious with other
men, like helping to start a new Christian radio station, helping a
friend win a seat on the school board, working at the local crisis
pregnancy center, or starting a men's group at your parish like

That Man Is You! or my friend Mark Houck's The King's Men? Or join our Bear's Man Cave, and we will help you start a small men's group (DeepAdventure.com).

At every sunset here in Waikiki, I look toward the ocean. A mile or so out, where the seas can be heavy, I see the teams in their outrigger canoes straining and training as they paddle their canoe together. Their rhythmic shouts can be heard at times across the ocean: "E lauhoe mai na wa`a; I ke ka, i ka hoe; i ka hoe, i ke ka; pae aku i ka `aina." It means "Paddle together, bail, paddle; paddle, bail; paddle towards the land."

When it comes to brothers helping each other, I especially like that word *bail*. When we are in over our heads sometimes, we need our brothers to help. Every outrigger canoe has a few buckets kicking around beneath the chairs of the paddlers because every canoe takes on water. When the seas get rough, bailing becomes more important than paddling. We need to be there for each other to paddle with each other—and, if need be, to bail each other out.

Tony Orband, my sidekick on *Long Ride Home*, once pulled up next to me at a stoplight in the freezing rain, somewhere near the ferry at Cape May, Maryland. He lifted his visor and, over the roar of the wind and the motorcycle engines, shouted to me, "Why do we love this?"

Bikers have a brotherhood forged just by knowing that the other has faced similar danger on the road. Just the fact that another biker is still there, riding kickstand up and rubber side down, says a lot about his endurance and skill.

When one biker pulls over on the side of the road, the next biker to come by will almost certainly stop to help. In my prideful- ness, this used to bother me. I just wanted to say, "Don't worry; I can handle this alone." But over time, I have become more than grateful for the brotherhood of bikers who are always there for each other, watching out for each other.

When we ride in a pack, everyone knows his role. At times, when there is a dangerous intersection ahead, a couple of designated bikers will ride on ahead to block traffic and make it safe for the others. When a biker sees a hazard, such as an object or divot in the road, he points at it with his boot or hand so the riders behind him are aware of it. We keep a tight pack on the freeways so that cars don't merge into our group. At the same time, we keep a safe distance from each other, we ride two by two but not next to each other. We ride staggered so we have time to react if something goes wrong with the biker in front of us.

We are a brotherhood. We ride together. We ride for each other. We watch out for each other, and we can count on each other. The dirt and grime that we have in common, as it collects on our gear and our faces, is thicker than blood.

Friendship with God is built the same way.

When you ride the trail with other men — not just on motorcycles, of course; I mean in everyday life — there grows a thickness to your relationship that goes beyond friendship and becomes brotherhood with the men who know you, who get you, and who have got your back. They're there in the best and worst of times. They cheer on your football team even though they're not fans. They know when you are down and could use a leg up back into the saddle, and they know when you just need a good kick in the butt.

When tough things go down, even if it is your own fault, they will stand there with you to help you right yourself and right the situation.

Be this to them.

Shoot straight and keep things *pono*; keep things right. Never talk behind another man's back. If someone has broken his word or betrayed you or let you down in some other way and you have something to say, say it directly to the man you have an issue with. In Hawaii, we call this *ho'oponopono*, making it right. Say what it is you have to say, to the person you need to say it to, and when you need to say it. Don't procrastinate. Then listen and put things right.

When my son broke his arm playing basketball, the doctor who reset it and put it in a cast told us, "When the bone heals, it will be stronger, not weaker. It will never break there again." *Ho'oponopono*, done right, should do this. Each man must own up to his own responsibility in the matter, and then, when the two do reconcile, they may have a stronger bond than ever.

The harvest is great, the laborers are few. Determined men working together, championing a common goal, not only make a significant impact, but they establish brotherhood. Bring your sons along with you in these endeavors and bring them with you when you are in the company of other men. When we hold our annual Man Cave Meet-Up Retreat we ask the men to bring their Confirmation-age and older sons with them.

In Hawaii, the men have a strong bond with one another. Because so much of our friendship, our brotherhood, is built out on and in the water, the ocean becomes the great equalizer. We don't think of who makes more money or who does what work or where someone lives. There is no peacocking. We think of enjoying the surf and the aloha. Here, it is very rare for men, when they first meet, to ask what the other person does for work. I cannot remember the last time that happened unless it is a haole or someone from the mainland. We value one another not so much for what we do for work but for who we *are* in terms of integrity and aloha and, of course, surfing.

In Hawaii, the younger men and women refer to any man at least twenty years older than they are as "Uncle." As I walk along the beach, the younger men call out, "Aloha, Uncle." That is the way of the Hawaiians. The older men are respected as uncles and are often looked to for help or advice by the younger men.

Part of the benefit of having a real brotherhood is that these brothers can help "uncle" our children. When a child acts out or does wrong, the uncles are there both to reprove him and love on him. When the child does well, they affirm him.

I once shared with a friend of mine a challenge I was having with one of my children. My friend happens to be a world champ surfer and is an enforcer in the water. He keeps things *pono* out there. A few months later, he was surfing the Banzai Pipeline, a very dangerous but epic surf reef, and he saw my son out there. He paddled over and said, "You can't be out here with us men. You go back and make things right with your dad." What my friend didn't know is that we'd already patched things over. But my son paddled in anyway, out of respect for the uncle. He called me from the beach, asking me to let the uncle know that everything was *pono*.

In the Mexican culture, there is a special relationship between two men that is called being compadres. This means that the men are godfathers to each other's children. That says it all, doesn't it? The band of brothers needs to be uncles and, in essence, to be godfathers to each other's children, especially to the young men.

My friend Fr. Bryce Lungren invited me to his next spring roundup. The local ranchers all take turns helping the others to round up their cattle out on the range, firing up the branding fire and branding the new calves, and doctoring the cattle that may need it.

There is a saying: "At a roundup, everyone is nineteen years old." Everyone, from the youngest to the oldest, has a role to play—and they'd better be spry. So it is in a brotherhood. Be there for each other, come hell or high water.

When things get tough, real men don't wait until the battle is over and then just step in to bayonet the wounded and tell them how they blew it. Real men step into the fray to help each other. When a brother falls, they pick him up.

When the ball is on the one-yard line, and the game clock is counting down and the fullback lowers his head and hits that line as hard as he can but is tackled for a loss, his teammates don't leave him there lying on his back. They reach down and pull him up. As they break the huddle, they look him in the eye and say, "You got this!"

In this time, now more than ever, we need true brotherhood. To that end, we have developed the Bear School of Manliness and Bear's Man Cave. Details can be found at DeepAdventure.com.

The Man Cave is a non-Facebook community on our own platform. It is a place for men to inspire one another, to seek prayer, and to develop friendships. We meet together through Zoom once a month or so, and we have an annual roundup for all the men around the country to come together.

The Man Cave is part of the School of Manliness with over two years of online video, audio, and written curriculum, with each month having titles similar to the chapter titles in this book. We all go through the same lesson together, as brothers. That lesson becomes the focus of our monthly Zoom meetup.

Each monthly lesson ends with a self-assessment that you can use to dig into where you are and where you want to go in that area of manly virtue. Men are encouraged to start their own local men's groups and use the tools on our site to lead them.

Fathers can get each of their sons his own unique login credentials to the School of Manliness so that fathers can lead their sons through it and even monitor their sons' progress. Once every week or so, fathers with their sons can view a couple of videos or listen to an audio lesson or read the written lesson and dig in and get some traction as they talk about manliness. The sons do not have access to the Man Cave Community site because they are too young.

We see ourselves as King David's Cave of Adullam. That is where David hid out with his men when Saul was hunting him to try to kill him. My friend Steve Ray is believed to have discovered this very cave on one of his more than one hundred forays to the Holy Land. He showed me one of the smooth, round stones hidden in the back of the cave that he found.

As David hid out there, men from all over Israel began to gather at the cave. The Bible tells us they were a band of misfits, men who were down on their luck or on the run from the law—or perhaps even their mothers-in-law. The men there formed each other as God formed them. In time, they became known as David's mighty men of valor. A small band of men can do great things. I have been to Thermopylae, where the three hundred Spartans fought. I have been to the valley where Gideon and his three hundred fought. They testify to us of what men can do when they stand together for each other and for their families.

The members of the Man Cave and School of Manliness are much the same. We are just a band of misfit knuckle draggers who have come together to be formed by each other and by God into His "mighty men of valor."

We encourage and help the men of the Man Cave to start their own local Man Cave of a dozen or so men who can gather for breakfast or coffee once a week or so or maybe sit on the back deck with a shot of whiskey and one of our Seven Virtues Cigars.

When we come together, we realize that we are all facing the same challenges, weaknesses, and patterns of sin. And we gain dignity in a certain transparency with each other when we share our worries and failings and then seek wisdom, guidance, prayer, and active support in overcoming our challenges.

You must search out good men and join with them. You will find that all men are facing the same temptations and dangers. "No temptation has overtaken you that is not common to man. God is faithful, and he will not let you be tempted beyond your strength, but with the temptation will also provide the way of escape, that you may be able to endure it" (1 Cor. 10:13). We are all tempted. Do you want to link up with those who are resisting or with those who are giving up? Do you and your friends gather under the battle standard of the Cross or under the white flag of surrender?

Jesus had His dozen. It is a good size for a small group. He also had His tight group of three friends to whom He gave nicknames: Simon He called Peter, and James and John He called the "Sons of Thunder." We also need our twelve friends and we need our closer set of three friends. In Hawaii, there is a saying in the outrigger paddling community: *Hoe pu me ka ikaika.* Paddle together strongly. We need other men in our canoe to propel us to virtue.

Do not let yourself be bothered by the inconsequential. One has only so much time in this world, so devote it to the work and the people most important to you, to

those you love and the things that matter.
One can waste half a lifetime with people
one doesn't really like, or doing things when
one would be better off somewhere else.

—Louis L'Amour, *Ride the River*

Rule 11

How a Man Treats a Woman Defines Him

He did not need anyone. I did not say that he
did not want someone. He told me that happiness
was born a twin, that it must be shared.

—Louis L'Amour, *The Lonesome Gods*

One thousand years ago, the Jewish philosopher Maimonides wrote a book called *The Guide for the Perplexed*. I picked up that book, naturally assuming that it must be about women. Wrong! That great philosopher did not even make an attempt to figure them out. Do not imagine that I have figured out everything there is to know about women. But here I go anyway.

This chapter is my attempt, as a battle-scarred and imperfect man, to share with you how to be a good man for a woman and how to find one who is worth cherishing, even laying down your life for.

How a man treats a woman—any woman, but especially "his woman"—defines him. Even though he may not have even met "his woman" yet, is he still faithful and devoted to her in all of his actions until he does find her? How does he treat his mom, his sisters, his female co-workers, his classmates, his restaurant server, the girl he is on a date with? This defines him as a man.

Saying that you love God is easy. There is no reality check there, at least until you die. But how you think of, speak of, and treat a woman is the litmus test that proves the durability of your love.

Perhaps it was because I was raised as the only son with three sisters that I saw the unique challenges and the unique heartaches that the women in my life went through.

I had lost touch with one of my college friends, Timothy McCormick, for more than thirty years. He is now a cast member on *Long Ride Home*. As we sat and had a whiskey together the night before the first shoot began, he made an interesting observation about me. He said, "The one thing I appreciated most about you back then was how you always spoke of women and treated women with respect."

If you want to find a good woman to accompany you, you must first be a good man. This whole book defines that path for you. John Wayne made it plain as day in the movie *McLintock!*: "To be a gentleman, you first got to be a man."

Living by your personal Creed and Code will get you fit for that special woman. She'll say yes to you instead of just passing you by. A woman is attracted to a strong, competent, confident man. I am not talking about a man with the kind of self-esteem that comes from his mommy. Even a little boy can have that. I am talking about manly confidence that only comes from competence earned through the diligent pursuit of excellence.

I have walked that path through a difficult marriage and then an annulment through the Catholic Church. I had to do my own suffering. I had to soak in the misery and do my own soul searching. I continued on in the best way that I knew how: I took care of my children and pursued my best life—until one day, many years later, I found a woman who somehow found me worthy of her. She takes my breath away. My bride, Cindy, is the best thing that has ever happened to me, and I hope she'd say the same of me.

When we first dated, and as she began slowly and carefully to open her heart to me, she introduced me to the Rascal Flatts song "Bless the Broken Road":

> Every long-lost dream led me to where you are.
> Others who broke my heart, they were like Northern
>   stars,
> Pointing me on my way into your loving arms.
> This much I know is true:
> That God blessed the broken road
> That led me straight to you.

The song speaks of lost dreams and broken hearts and failed relationships—but how all that suffering is worth it because it led to his wife's loving arms. (By the way, a certain brokenness is almost prerequisite to serving the Lord.)

Cindy and I are all in. We are for each other. And it remains a mystery and a wonder to me to this day that we found each other, even though we lived five thousand miles apart—and all in God's timing. Years before we met, she had stayed in a hotel room one hundred yards away from my condo lanai. We were so close to meeting, we could almost have reached out and touched each other. Only the Catholic Church that was situated between the two buildings kept us at a distance. Now it has sacramentally joined us.

I was contemplating those broken roads and broken relationships a while ago, and a math equation came to me. You know all those years when you asked your math teacher, "When will

I need this in real life?" Well, at least in this one instance, it led to a breakthrough for me. Thank you, fifth-grade math teacher.

Marriage is intended for two people to come together to become one. In Mark 10:8, Jesus quotes Genesis 2:24: "The two shall become one." Sounds a bit like a simple math equation. Let's check it out.

The formula for marriage is not $1 + 1 = 2$. That is just two people living together but having their own separate lives; sharing the same bed, but living as roommates. They never share a bank account or dreams or desires or perhaps even have children. It is not a marriage. It is an arrangement. The Catholic Church teaches that a marriage takes two emotionally healthy people devoted to each other and freely giving themselves and willing the true good for the other in love. Remember, it takes two becoming one to be a marriage.

Marriage is not $1 \times 0 = 0$ either. It does not work if one person is giving his or her all but the other one is not willing to give his or her love fully. It takes two autonomous people with healthy identities giving all of themselves to make a marriage. Otherwise, they are just bartering for affection.

The marriage equation is the mathematical "unitary" principle of $1 \times 1 = 1$. You see, the number 1 in math is considered a "unity identity." It takes two individual people with healthy identities to come together in unity to make one marriage, to make one new identity.

Do you see that with the Holy Trinity, it is somewhat this way too? $1 \times 1 \times 1 = 1$—that is, three Persons with one essence. It is from God that we receive our identity, for we are the *imago Dei*. We are made in God's image, and it is in knowing and embracing our God-given identity that we become the persons we were created to be.

When a man and a woman become one in marriage, they are, in some special sense, an imitation of the Trinity. So it is that the Catholic Church has the man and the woman express this in the marriage vows:

Priest: Have you come here to enter into Marriage without coercion, freely and wholeheartedly?

Are you prepared, as you follow the path of Marriage, to love and honor each other for as long as you both shall live?

Are you prepared to accept children lovingly from God and to bring them up according to the law of Christ and His Church?

Bride and groom: I am.

Priest: [Name], do you take [Name] to be your wife? Do you promise to be faithful to her in good times and in bad, in sickness and in health, to love her and to honor her all the days of your life?

Groom: I do.

Marriage is meant to be for a lifetime. Perhaps the Apache "squaw-taking ceremony" makes it even simpler to understand. They just say one word to each other: *Varlebena*. It simply means "forever."

Randy Travis sang the same thing in his song "Forever and Ever, Amen"—that marriage is meant to be for a lifetime:

> You may think that I'm talking foolish.
> You've heard that I'm wild and free.
> You may wonder how I can promise you now
> This love that I feel for you always will be.

But you're not just time that I'm killin'.
I'm no longer one of those guys,
As long as I live, this love that I give
Is gonna be yours until the day that I die.
Oh baby, I'm gonna love you forever,
Forever and ever, amen.

Many years after my annulment, I finally arrived at a place of healing and total rest and trust in God. I was happy in my life. I had plenty of time to work, play, pray, and study. I was an empty nester. I was very happy to be alone. I had discovered the writings of the early Church Fathers and the saints and the new *Catechism of the Catholic Church*. I was captivated with the Truth that I was learning, and I was growing in intimacy with God as I returned to the Catholic Church. I had always had a deep faith, but it seemed that I had been swimming in the shallow end of the pool. Now it seemed that the breadth and depth of an ocean of Catholic Truth was there for me to dive into.

I was very happy just to sit on the beach at sunset with a cigar and a shot of whiskey and spend time with these new friends of mine, these ancient writers, reading their works, asking them to pray for me and to help me understand more deeply the truths that they shared. I was so joyful to fellowship with them and the truth that I found in their writings. It seemed that, as I read down on the beach as the sun set and the stars blinked on and rotated in the sky, that the hours slipped by as I soaked up an understanding of Catholic doctrine, morality, and the spiritual journey, and I would just slip into contemplative prayer.

I was happy and free and with no encumbrances of a rela-tionship, I could spend hours every day in prayer and study. My identity in Christ was being informed and formed through the trials of life, Catholic teaching, and, most especially, God's ever-present and unmerited grace.

I really did not need to be with someone. I had become a Benedictine Oblate and I even contemplated just living on alone in the joy that I had. Yet I desired to share my happiness with a woman—one who would add to, not subtract from, my serenity and bliss.

That miracle happened on Easter Sunday morning in 2015 on a beach in Indialantic, Florida, five thousand miles from my home in Waikiki.

Fourteen years earlier, I had pedaled my bicycle from the beach in San Diego, California, to the shores of Jacksonville, Florida. I pursued that adventure with two things in my mind and in my heart. First, that journey was my goodbye to the mainland. I would move to Hawaii as soon as I returned to California. Second, that whole trip was a dedicated prayer for that special woman I hadn't met yet. I asked God to bless her and protect her and to help us find each other.

Now, in 2015, I had arrived on the beach early, in total darkness, before that Easter sunrise Mass. As the first light began to show, I came to realize that the crowd had filled in and I was surrounded by thousands of worshippers. Yet, though I was with so many people, at that moment, I felt particularly alone. After Mass, I drove fourteen miles up the coast to Cocoa Beach with my tandem surfboard on the surf rack on top of the car. I was heading to lead a tandem surfing "Expression Session" in the legendary Dick Catri's Easter Surf Contest.

I carried my big twelve-foot tandem board down to the beach and sat it down in front of the announcer's stand, waiting for our exhibition to begin. My good friend Eileen Lundy, who always traveled with the tandem teams around the world and was our announcer, spotted me. I heard her announce from the stand, "World Champ Bear Woznick is on the beach to teach tandem surfing if anyone wants to learn."

It was as if the Red Sea parted, and suddenly there she stood. She jumped up and down: "Pick me! Pick me!" You see, unbeknownst to me, this beautiful, athletic woman had been coming down to watch us tandem-surf, whenever we came to town, for over seven years.

Sunday was her only day to call her own and she would drive from Orlando to Cocoa Beach just to soak up the sun and the waves. She had fallen in love with the sport of tandem surfing and had so badly wanted to try it, but her life circumstances had not let her. Her mother was suffering from stage-four cancer, and she was her only caregiver. She was also raising her teenage niece, whose mother had died.

She had no real life of her own. She worked to provide and care for her mom and her niece. But now her mother, after eight years of suffering, had recently passed away. Her niece, CeeJay, had now grown up and was out of the house. For the first time in eight years, she was her own woman. And so it was that, on that particular Easter Sunday morning, nothing could hold her back from learning to tandem-surf. She leaped at the chance.

This chapter could just as easily be called: "Tandem Surfing and the Art of Loving a Woman." You see, I met my bride that day, and, in time, we fell in love on my tandem surfboard.

That Easter morning, I taught her to do a few lifts and then teamed Cindy up with a guy there who had said he was a tandem surfer. I watched over them as they paddled out, and, in fact, he was able to put her into an easy lift, a cradle—that is, he lifted her in his arms as a man does when he carries his bride across the threshold.

They were both excited, and they decided to form a team to prepare for the National Kidney Foundation Labor Day contest, which would be held four months later in the same town. I had been renting a condo on the beach, as I was working on filming TV shows for EWTN, so I was able to meet them down on the beach once or twice a week to train them.

I realized right away that he was not a very good surfer. He did not do a good job of positioning himself in the lineup, selecting the wave, or catching the wave. Then, as he struggled to ride it, he would attempt to lift her. Usually, he'd wipe out; quite often, that meant he fell on top of her, on the board. Worse, she might be dropped into the water and risk hitting her head on the board or in the sand of the shallow water.

But through all of this, I saw a brave, happy, valiant woman who never let her tandem partner feel small and did all she could to help him to succeed, even to the point of helping him to carry the heavy tandem surfboard to and from the beach. I started to call her "TC"—short for "Tough Chick." She had been a rodeo barrel racer and trick rider. She was a skydiver, a scuba diver, and a snowboarder, and she could barefoot water-ski. She was light, athletic, and flexible. She was a natural tandem girl.

One day, as we walked to my condo to watch the video of the two of them surfing, she held back a bit to take a phone call from one of her girlfriends; it sounded as though her friend was having a tough time with her husband—who, it turns out, had been cheating on her. Cindy walked into the condo looking sad and frustrated, and she just let her emotions tumble out. "Someday, somewhere," she said, "some man has to teach men to be men again."

I looked at her in shock and answered her, "You don't know what I do, do you?"

"No." She meekly responded, a little surprised by her own outburst.

"That is what I do. I challenge men to be virtuous." I gave her a copy of one of my books. The next time I saw her, she had read a good portion of the book, and I could tell it was reaching her in a deep way. It seems that, at the moment of that outburst, God joined Cindy's heart to mine in my outreach to men. Yeah, God! Holy Spirit Action Plan!

At some point, I had a chance to talk with her for a moment alone, and I told her straight out, "Your tandem partner keeps dropping you, and you are getting hurt. His number-one job is to protect you. I want to tell him that he should not surf with you anymore until he takes surf lessons and becomes a better surfer."

I was getting angry. He had no business putting her in harm's way. She responded that she had already told him the same thing but that he wanted to try one more time.

The next week, I saw them walking down to the beach again, so I grabbed my tandem board, paddled out a hundred yards away, and kept an eye on them. When they caught the first wave, he stood up awkwardly and then attempted to lift her as his board grabbed a rail. He fell down on top of her as she hit the board. I watched her get up and rub her shoulder. She turned her back to him as she walked to the beach. She did not want him to see that she was tearing up.

She always protected his dignity when he failed. But this time, she did not turn to walk back out to the waves and try again. This time, she walked toward the beach. I could tell that she was not only in physical pain: she was brokenhearted, as she so much desired to be a tandem girl.

I walked toward her, carrying my tandem board, and waved for her to come to me. I ignored her tandem partner because he had not protected her. My focus was only on her. She looked at me as I said, "Do you want to paddle out with me?"

Her eyes lit up. "Yes, please!" We paddled out, and on three consecutive waves, we did three different overhead lifts. When we came in, her tandem partner was long gone. I asked her if she would be my tandem partner in the contest, which was now just six weeks away. Her eyes lit up as only her beautiful green eyes can do, and again she said, "Yes, please!" As we surfed together, I learned that power is beautiful, and I saw that she was both.

We grew to know each other and respect each other on that surfboard. In time, we fell in love. I asked her to marry me a year and a half later in Monterey Bay, where I was raised. I knelt down near the Lone Cypress on the Seventeen Mile Drive by Pebble Beach Golf Course and asked her to be my bride. Once again, she said, "Yes, please!" She knelt down to lift me up. We kissed and held each other and thanked God for all the broken roads that had led us together.

Two years later, we had a betrothal ceremony at St. Elijah Monastery on the highest peak on the Greek Island of Santorini. Then, nine months later, the day after she became a Catholic, we were married at Holy Name of Jesus Catholic Church in Indialantic, Florida. Thank you, Fr. Scott Circe. (Fr. Scott, in time, became a cast member on *Long Ride Home*.)

The best way I know how to describe a man and woman in love is to use tandem surfing as an analogy, so please excuse me as I step away from the cowboy theme. As we all love to say: "You can lead a horse to water, but you can't make it surf."

The man's role in tandem surfing is much like the role of a man in a marriage. He is the captain of the ship. The captain's number-one role is to protect the souls on his ship, and so it is that a tandem man's first priority is to protect the woman. He determines where to wait for the waves. He chooses which wave to surf. He decides the timing of the paddle-in. Then, with her lying down in front, he gets up first, and she gets up. He lifts her and draws her back to him so that they are connected as she rests her back against his chest and her cheek against his, with her knees slightly bent, totally responsive, as she stands with her feet within the span of his feet.

The two surf as though they are one with each other and with the wave. It is the same in a marriage, in which the two become one with each other and with God.

As they surf along the face of that wave, he signals to her, and she leaps as he lifts her into one of about fifty lifts. His first priority is to protect her and then it is to display her power, beauty, and grace as he holds her in extreme, beautiful poses.

It may well be the most awe-inspiring sport in the world, but it is also particularly dangerous to the woman. She is held high overhead while the man carves the face of waves that are usually at least six feet high, sometimes much higher. The man's first priority therefore must be both to protect her and inspire and earn her trust. Without her trust, nothing can work.

I have scars on my back from being dragged across the reef. When I anticipate an imminent wipeout, in order to protect the woman, I bring her out of the lift, cradle her against my chest, and jump backward off the board to protect her from the reef, our surfboard, and the falling lip of the wave. I am tethered to the board with my surf leash, so at times the board drags me across the razor-sharp reef. My shins look like an amusement park, too, from other surfers dropping in on us and banging their boards against my legs as I continue to hold her up high in a lift and surf through the mayhem, protecting her so that she does not get hurt.

All men who tandem-surf protect their women. The sport requires a certain physical closeness when paddling on the board and when doing lifts, so if a man does not respect and protect a woman's dignity as well as her physical safety, the word gets out pretty fast along the coconut telegraph and women know to avoid him.

Through all of our years of tandem surfing, Cindy has taken only one really hard wipeout. That was only a few weeks ago at the Duke Ocean Fest here in Waikiki, on a sixteen-foot day when we had to use our backup competition board because our big-wave tandem board had been "borrowed" by someone. I thoroughly enjoyed the wipeout. There's nothing like a good back adjustment. But Cindy got stuffed pretty bad. Yet, being the valiant woman that she is, she got back on the board and paddled out with me again, and we surfed together as well as we ever had.

It seems in life these days that men don't protect and inspire trust in a woman anymore. Most of them do not see that it is their role to lift a woman up so that her strength and her beauty can be seen. The rise of a woman to her full beauty and potential is not the downfall of men; in fact, it is one of my highest purposes as a man: to lift women up, to help them flourish.

When we surf together, especially in big waves, Cindy needs to be able to trust me, but I need to trust in her too. I need to know that she is not going to bail on me or overreact or do something unexpected that is not consistent with our training. If she is second-guessing me, I cannot take care of either of us.

This is the way the marriage of a man and woman should be. Each trusts the other. Each does what he or she does best. Each gives his or her all. Each experiences the thrill of life in a way that he or she never could without being in that devoted marriage.

On the surfboard, there is a complementarity between a man and a woman. We each have our roles, and when we do them right, we surf as one. It is the same way in a marriage. We have different natures, mentally and emotionally but also physically. A man and a woman complement each other in their physical nature; you can see that not only are they unique but that they definitely go together. By nature itself, it is obvious that it is intended for a man and a woman to become one flesh. In the same way, their souls complement each other. They are meant to complete each other.

Men are made from mud, but women are more highly refined, for God formed the woman from Adam's rib. God took her from right there next to his heart, and so a man's and a woman's hearts are to be one. In this same way, the Bride of Christ came forth on the Cross when blood and water flowed from the side of Christ.

A marriage is sacred, for a married couple is an icon of Christ and His Church. " 'For this reason a man shall leave his father and mother and be joined to his wife, and the two shall become one flesh.' This is a great mystery, and I mean in reference to Christ and the church" (Eph. 5:31–32).

One day, as we were sitting on the beach having our morning cup of coffee, I asked my bride, "What is it women want?" Her instant response was, "Everything." She laughed a bit, but then she said, "But it's true. They want their man to be all in."

Not long ago, I was the guest on a Zoom call with about thirty young Catholic singles. The group had advertised my subject as "Christian Masculinity," and when they introduced me that way, my response was visceral. "No," I firmly said. "I am not here to talk about masculinity. I am here to talk with you about manliness."

This was set up as a two-way Zoom call so the men and women could all participate with me. I was appalled that a lot of the viewers, especially the male viewers, did not have their cameras on so that they could be seen. I encouraged them all to turn on their screen so we could all see each other. One by one, the women clicked on but only a few men.

I coaxed the men again, with little response. I finally flat-out told them, if you are so passive a male that you cannot turn on your video for us to see you, then you should just exit this session. One by one, most of the men clicked on, and a few left the call.

As I began to discuss with them Rules for Manliness, I could see that something was stirring in the men and the women. So I turned the tables and asked the women a question about what they want to see in a man. The women said, straight out, that they need men to be men. "We are tired of nice guys. We need them to be bold and to be strong for us, to show some leadership and not be so passive. We want them to ask us out on a date or—how about this?—even ask us to marry them." All of them indicated that they had just about given up on finding a real man, and some asked if they should just settle. To which my emphatic response was "No!"

A real man treats a woman not as someone lesser than he but as someone worthy of his respect. Boys use women. Boys abuse women. Gentlemen treat women with dignity.

Not long ago, I arrived to speak at a young adult Theology on Tap gathering held at a small pizza joint. Before I could even order a beer, my bride and I were cornered by several young women speaking to us in a somewhat hushed way. "There are a lot of nice guys here, but none of them ask us out on dates—or, if we do date for a while, they never mention marriage. We want to be with a Christian man, but we have had it with these nice guys who never step up their game."

A sissified, passive, neutered nice guy can't be the man a woman wants or can trust herself to. She knows that he can't fulfill the mission that God intends for him as a husband or a father unless he develops a spine. He cannot fulfill the longing in a woman for a real man or in a child for a real father—or in society as primary protector, provider, procreator, and priest in the home.

It is often said that young women are attracted to the bad boy. Emphasis on the word *boy*. They may not realize it, but what they really are looking for is a strong, tough, powerful man who will stand by them and stand up for them not a macho misogynistic jerk.

Women know instinctively that there is a difference between a nice guy and a good man. While the nice guy may be helpful, while he may be pleasant company and might never offend anyone, they are passive. When push comes to shove, they never push back. Women also know, way down in their knower, that when push comes to shove, they want a man they can rely on—a man with a backbone, determination, competence, confidence, and grit; a man who will work to better himself and improve the lives of those around him; a man who will do the right thing, come hell or high water, no matter the personal sacrifice.

Women push the nice guy aside and put him in the friend zone while they wait for someone with manly virtue. They want a man of principle, who knows who he is and where he is going. And, guys, if you meet a woman and she wants anything *less* than this, she is not the woman for you.

Your course is this: pursue manly virtue and prepare for that adventure with a woman.

About six months into our relationship, Cindy casually threw out a little hint with all the subtlety of a cowgirl throwing out a lasso to haul in a wild mustang. A song came on the radio, and she reached over, as she likes to do, and turned it up. Beyoncé belted out the lyrics: "If you like it, then you should've put a ring on it."

Well played, I thought. I started looking for a ring.

The Holy Spirit's word to men today is the same word that the angel of the Lord spoke to St. Joseph two thousand years ago: "Do not fear to take Mary as your wife" (Matt. 1:20).

So many men today are afraid to be married. They say that the woman will marry and then divorce them and take their money and their children with her. The worry is valid. I understand. But that only means you have to be prudent in choosing whom you date. Discern her character as you go along. But when you find a good woman and fall in love, "do not be afraid."

These days, man-boys are too cowardly to man up and enter into marriage. To put it crudely, in high school there were those girls who would date guys, make out with them a bit, and string them along but who would not "put out." The high school boys all called girls like that a tease. The women were right, of course, to draw the line at some point before sexual intimacy. But what I am saying is that a man-boy who strings a girl along, talks about marriage someday (maybe), or moves in with her but never marries her, is like a coquettish high school girl. He is the biggest tease of all.

What can be more twisted and evil than a cavalier attitude toward love, sex, and marriage? Disordered sexual intimacy can be more destructive than the atomic fission of a nuclear bomb, but properly ordered sexual intimacy in the context of a nuptial union can be more powerful and creative than the nuclear fusion of two atoms.

St. John Paul II wrote more than 130 homilies on what has come to be called the Theology of the Body. His writings emphasized that love and responsibility go hand in hand.

Men, you must get this right.

Sexual union is not just pleasure. In a sense, it is as if a part of a person's soul clings to that other person. The more sexual partners someone has, the more his soul is colonized by bits and pieces of those memories that restrict the true intimacy he seeks.

When a man-boy has sex with a woman with no regard for the procreative and unitive elements, he is taking no responsibility for her heart and for the life of the potential baby. A man-boy seeks only his own pleasure and views women as objects—a means to an end and not as the subject of his love and self-donation.

Men, how you treat women defines you. As with all virtue, the battle begins with your inner life. Do not let your mind dwell on lustful thoughts. Do not look at pornography. Do not hang out with men who speak lustfully and disrespectfully of women.

Women who choose to move in with a man before marriage usually do so because they see it as a pathway to marriage, but the divorce rate for couples who lived together before eventually marrying is 30 percent higher than for those who don't. Man-boys trade in their relationships as they would a car.

It is also a fact that couples who are married have a much happier sex life. Of course they do! Their sexual union is a sharing of souls. Those who are married have given themselves to each other, so they experience a deeper pleasure and joy in bed.

Having said all that, just how does a man choose the right woman? A man should consider that thought seriously. I suggest that a man actually write down the qualities he would choose in a woman he would consider falling madly in love with.

Be aware of what a good woman is and isn't. There is a cowboy saying: "A horse that bucks will always buck. It might be weeks or months, but the horse that bucks cannot be trusted." When a horse bucks, it is angry and wants to hurt you.

When you see a woman who is manipulative, or is passive-aggressive, or has angry outbursts, take it as a serious warning. It is not your job to fix her.

Be wary of an abusive or angry woman. If you feel as if you are walking on pins and needles around her, you probably are. It's time to move on before things get serious.

Coming out of a long, lonely marriage, I really desired the kind of marriage that my Mom and Dad had, so I asked them what I should look for in a woman. My mother said it simply: "Next time, you need to find a strong woman. It takes two healthy, strong people to make a marriage and two people who give themselves to each other wholeheartedly. I know you want to be the white knight and protect and provide for a woman. It's deeply in your nature. I can see it. But find a strong woman who can really love you, too, and not just be needy and take from you."

In the West, the woman wasn't just the useless, pretty toy that some men seem to be attracted to these days. She had physical strength as well as strength of character. She could handle a gun, and she could handle trouble. So many men these days hide trouble from a woman. But that is not honest or fair, and it is disrespectful to the strength that God has given her. As a CPA, I have seen when a man hides financial challenges from his wife until suddenly the dam bursts. By keeping secrets from her, this man dishonors his wife. What's more, a good woman's wisdom in times like this can be a great help to a man.

Louis L'Amour said, "There are men who prefer to keep trouble from a woman, but it seems to me that is neither reasonable nor wise. I've always respected the thinking of women, and also their ability to face up to trouble when it comes, and it shouldn't be allowed to come on them unexpected." L'Amour wrote about strong women. They were determined and courageous, but just like even the most powerful among us, from time to time, they found themselves in a vulnerable position, whether it was due to the elements or to bad men with bad intentions.

This is where the cowboy hero rides in to make a stand with her. Maybe there is a love connection; maybe not. But the cowboy stands between her and the danger of a coming winter or of a greedy cattleman wanting her ranch or wanting her or wanting her *and* her ranch.

While taking both of my black-belt tests, I got serious leg injuries. For the first one, I had a torn meniscus and, for the second one, a torn calf muscle. For the first time, I felt I was not ready to take on the biggest bully on the block. Being strong, highly skilled, and determined may not be enough in a real fight. I was a strong but vulnerable man. Do you see what I mean? A strong woman still may be in need of a strong man to protect and provide for her, especially when the marriage bed brings children.

You may want to find things like this to write down on your list of the qualities of the right woman for you. Find a woman who respects or even adores her father, one who actually likes men. Find a woman with courageous happiness, for that shows strength of character. Find a woman who is comfortable with herself as a woman, who does not need to strive to be the man in the relationship or compete with him. Find a woman who is playful, faithful, and steps up to the plate when something needs to be done.

Find a woman who is gracious, who is not quick to anger, and who is hospitable to all. One of the surest signs of a good woman is that she remembers other people's birthdays. In other words, she genuinely cares about others. Find a woman who drives you just a bit crazy when it comes to sexual desire. Find a woman who is proud to stand beside you, walk beside you, and perhaps even lean on you a bit.

Here is my "guide for the perplexed" when it comes to dating. You can find out in just the first couple of dates if a woman is someone you might just possibly want to marry. If not, then end it. But if it looks hopeful, then keep seeing her.

Then the hundred-day rule kicks in. After one hundred days, if she has been holding back her true self, she will begin to let her guard down and let you see more clearly who she really is. Do not put her on a pedestal. Men like to project on a woman attributes that they wish she has but she really doesn't. Discover who she really is.

After one hundred days, the relationship should be at a point where you are considering that she could be the one for you to marry. If, at any time, you realize that she is not for you, you cannot string her along. Man up and tell her.

In a year, you should know if she is the one for you to marry. Pull the trigger and ask her. Soon after that, set the wedding date, and then marry within a year of being engaged.

Part of the reason for this all to be only a two-year process is that the fire of sexual desire will burn, and you need to refrain from making love until you are married. It was not easy, but I was a virgin on my wedding night. Stay chaste. Show her that your love can wait.

Here is Christ's great call and challenge to us men: "Love your wife as Christ loves the Church." For the Church is the Bride of Christ. And how did Christ love His Bride? By laying His life down for her. That ought to make you choke on your beef jerky. Be faithful to your wife. Be devoted, not just committed. Cherish her.

Not once in his more than one hundred westerns did one of Louis L'Amour's cowboy's lust after a woman and cross that sacred line before marriage.

To be respected, a woman must first respect herself. The great breakdown in manliness and in society began when the "Pill-liberated woman," and, if not that, then the local abortion mill, could take care of the problem. They could have sex whenever they wanted, with whomever they wanted, and men began to pressure them even more. They broke their social contract with other women to wait until marriage. It made it easier to resist a man's advances when a woman knew that other women were holding men to that high standard of waiting until marriage.

Man-boys in this "swipe right, swipe left," hookup culture play games of catch and release or they pressure girls to have sex with them. "If you really loved me, you would sleep with me." They are using girls.

Today a woman may easily feel that, if she says no to a man, she may not ever have *any* man in her life. Why should he wait to have sex when he can get what he wants from another woman?

Why? Because a real man, a good man, will wait.

Here is a lesson that I learned from hibiscus flowers. My mom first pointed out something about them while we sat on the lanai on the island of Molokai. It was something that I never noticed. She said, "They are one-day flowers."

The hibiscus flower blossoms as the sun rises and shows forth its wild beauty throughout the day until sunset. As the sun goes down, it closes up. It lasts for only one day. And so it is with loving a woman. Renew your love for her each day, by listening to her, helping her, cherishing her, caring about what she cares about.

Each morning after our coffee, and after I pray for Cindy's wildest dreams to come true, I pick a hibiscus flower and give it to her. In fact, we are about to head out for that morning walk and swim right now. She always acts as if it is the sweetest thing that I have ever done for her. She brings it home and places it in a special glass of water, where it shows its full beauty until it fades after sunset. But Cindy knows there will be a new expression of love from me in the morning—and not just in the flower, but in every moment.

Learn the lesson of the hibiscus. Be courageous enough to tenderly love your wife.

"The Apache don't have a word for love," he said. "Know what they both say at the marriage? The squaw-taking ceremony?"

"Tell me."

"Varlebena. It means forever. That's all they say."

—Louis L'Amour, *Hondo*

Rule 12

Fill Your Quiver: The Adventure of Fatherhood

He had been the best of fathers and it was never easy to be a father to strong sons ... each coming to manhood, each asserting himself, loving the father yet wishing to be free of him.... So it has been since the world began, for the young do not remain young and the time must come when each must go out on his own grass.

—Louis L'Amour, *Jubal Sackett*

Now and again, a good, solid man approaches me at an event with a look of consternation and says, "Sometimes I feel really torn between the life of adventure like you have—of hitting the road on my motorcycle, or sailing beyond the horizon, or gutting it out and disappearing into the Rockies on horseback—but I have a family."

My response is simple: "Being a father is about the greatest adventure that any man can have." (This is especially true, of course, for those called to be priests, for a priest is a father to his whole parish.)

What is a father? He is a bucket of grit, fortitude, know-how, and worry, mingled with hopeful determination that he will give his children the best home possible and the best possible start in pursuing a rich, beautiful, well-lived life—a life that will go on forever.

As he shoulders the responsibility to care for his bride and their children, with all the hopes and worries that go along with that, he goes from not even knowing how to hold a baby to holding the whole future of a child in his hands. He grows into his fatherhood and into his manhood. As he holds his own newborn boy in the palm of his hands, he becomes a man. He has to man up. His family is counting on him—and you know what? He likes it.

When he becomes a new father, his life priorities are transformed. It is no longer just about him: it is about his family. His wife counts on him now more than ever, and his children need him to be all in, and so he makes choices about work and friends and play that he would not otherwise have made, because his bride and his children are counting on him. I remember surfing Rincon in central California, on a big day when I was thirty-one and had two children. For the first time in my life, I hesitated on a big wave, thinking, "Who will take care of my family if I get hurt?"

Little things change, big things change, and something powerful emerges in the heart of a man when he becomes a father.

One afternoon, in my junior year of high school, I started to doze in class. You would have too. I had just moved from Santa Cruz, California, to Waco, Texas. I was in a food coma, thanks to a lunch of tater tots, grisly chicken-fried steak (whatever that was), and a large Dr. Pepper. The drone of the voice of the most boring history teacher in history caused my thoughts to drift off.

Suddenly, something struck me like an epiphany. Out of the blue, the thought came to me that, one day, I could become a father. It was a tectonic shift, a restructuring of my soul and the trajectory of my whole life. The awareness that I could be part of bringing a new human being into the world blew me away. I was blown right out of my saddle. Every decision from that moment until now has been made with that in the forefront of my mind: the adventure of fatherhood.

I found myself saying no to drinking and smoking and the parties that went along with it. I worked after school and on weekends through high school and college and graduated with hardly any student debt. In college, I chose courses that I was naturally drawn to but also that I thought would open doors to a good-paying career so I could support my family. I had not even met the woman who would be the mother of my children, but I was already faithful to her and to my children. I was making decisions for her good and for the good of our children.

To be called "father" is an awesome honor and responsibility, for we call the first Person of the Holy Trinity "Father." We don't call him Father just because He is kind of like an earthly dad. No. It is the other way around. God is a Father, and we who are earthly fathers are to imitate Him, to be like Him, to be icons of Him in this world.

The Bible tells us that God is love. Love protects. Love provides. But love does one more thing: love procreates. God the Father eternally begat His Son, the second Person of the Holy Trinity, and the Holy Spirit is the love that proceeds from the Father and the Son, for "God is love" (1 John 4:8).

A Father Procreates

God the Father gives us men the great dignity of procreating, of fathering a human being. At the moment of conception, God infuses a fresh, new, unique, spiritual, rational soul into that child's body. That child becomes both God's child and yours. That child, with your example and guidance, is meant to know God and love Him back. That child is your child, but he is also meant to be your brother or sister in Christ.

Never forget this. That child is an *imago Dei*, made in God's likeness as well as in yours. God is that child's Father too. That should bring you some hope and strength. God will be there to help you. But also remember that that child is His. That child is sacred to Him. Treat your child as the sacred person he or she is.

What an incredible honor and adventure it is to be a father. The awakening of this part of our being also inspires in us a newfound deeper respect for our own parents.

Fathers are not replaceable. The absence of the father is devastating to a family. The feminist movement and the woke culture's efforts to minimize the role of men as the social construct of the nanny state have hijacked the family, to the children's detriment.

It does not take a village to raise a child, as some say. First and foremost, it takes a mom and a dad.

There was a study done many years ago about the impact that parents have on their children's continuing in their faith when they grow up. When only the mom brings children up in the faith, about one-third continue in that faith. When both the mother and father are devoted to bringing up their children in the faith, more like three-fourths stay in that faith. But what is astounding is that when it is only the father who raises the children in the faith, the number drops very little from that 75 percent. The impact of men leading their children by example in the pursuit of their faith is immense.

The ancient Hawaiian navigators had a way of crossing the swift and dangerous channels between the islands that lie beyond the horizon, out of view. They would build two fires. One was built high up on a mountain and then another farther down. As the men sailed away, if they kept the sighting of the lower fire directly beneath the one that was up above, they knew they were on a direct course to the other island.

As they sailed and the two fires began to dip beneath the distant horizon, they would continue until they would begin to see fire on the mountaintop of the island that they were sailing toward. As they sailed toward that fire, the lower fire would eventually come into view. Then they would align that top fire with the one below it, and they would safely find their course and make their way to the safe harbor of the other island.

This is the same way we surfers find our lineups when we are out a mile or so, surfing bigger waves. We look for two well-known markers on the land—perhaps a cell tower in the distance and a hotel elevator shaft closer to shore. When we line those up, we know we're at the spot where the next big set will break. Sailors do this too.

So it is in our families. The father is that bright fire on the highest place on the mountain. He is always looking out, alert for opportunity and danger. The mother is that fire that burns just as bright and is closer to the sea and is the first to welcome people as they arrive. A father and mother who are in agreement in raising their children and in agreement with the Lord set their children on a solid heading as they sail the seas of life.

Do your best to come to agreement with your wife on decisions concerning raising your children. If a husband and wife can't come to agreement on rearing the children, it breeds chaos, confusion, and rebellion.

I was at a Napa Institute gathering a few years back, and during the session with Archbishop Charles Chaput, someone asked him, "What do you think is the most effective evangeliza-tion program out there today?" His response was immediate and rocked the room with its truthfulness: "Get married. Have lots of children. Raise them up in the Lord." Love procreates a new generation of saints. Think of that. We Christians are meant to populate Heaven.

A Father Protects

Around five hundred years before Christ, the prophet Nehemiah returned to Jerusalem from exile in Persia. He was shocked to see the breach and the decay in the temple walls. He challenged the fathers of Israel to rebuild the walls. Starting in chapter 3 of Nehemiah, we see a running list of men who each led his family, his own "domestic church," in working to restore a specific sec-tion of the wall. Each man worked to build a wall of protection even as today fathers need to join together to help each other to do the same.

In Nehemiah, each man carried a drawn sword as he car-ried supplies along the construction site, and while he worked, another man stood guard over him with a spear and a shield. If there was an attack on one side of the wall, they would blow the ram's horn, and men would come running to help. This is what fathers need today. We need brothers who will stand with us as together we rebuild our families and join them together.

There is a breach in the wall of our society today, and it runs right through the living room of every home. The enemy has entered in by the Trojan horse of iPhones, liberal schools, and media. There is a saying: "Do not look a gift horse in the mouth." Today we should add, "Do not look a gift horse at the other end, either" because social media is just a load of horseplop. It is the father who must reject this invasion into his home and build that wall back up. Love protects. The man must step up and lead his family, his domestic church, and rebuild that wall with solid teaching and love and bring healing to our land.

What the world needs more than anything is just, plain and simply, real fathers.

If this world is ever going to get set back on its axis, it's going to take fathers who love and cherish their daughters and sons and show them what it means to be secure in a father's love. That love will infuse within their children moral courage and virtue.

So many children are born into a fatherless wasteland. Out-of-wedlock births are at record highs. Yet even two-parent homes can be effectively fatherless. The dad vacates the house either by being married more to his career than to his family or by focusing more on having fun than with his *kuleana* to his children. Some even physically abandon their children entirely. The vacuum that an absent father leave fills with demons. It leaves sons and daughters to be raised by a woman who hates men because of how she was betrayed by one. It breeds confusion and chaos, especially in boys.

Do you know what is even worse than that? It's the unmarried father who says to his pregnant girlfriend these poisonous, cowardly words: "I know you need to make a choice, and I will support you 100 percent, no matter what you decide." At that moment, what she really needs to hear that man say is this: "I am responsible. I will stand by you as you have this child, and I will be a father to that child, and support that child, regardless of whether we marry." If someone is man enough to conceive a child, he had better be man enough to be a father to that child. Baby murder is not an option.

St. John Paul II's first writings were on "love and responsibility." Nothing will make a boy into a man faster than protecting and providing for a mother and their child. When a man has this *kuleana*, it is time to cowboy up.

Do you want your family to respect you? Then first you must respect, in both your words and actions, your God-given authority. You must first lead by example and show in your heart that you ride for the brand. You don't want to force your family or drive them to do what you want. That never works. But if you lead them by the example of your integrity and lay down your life for them, they may just follow. In fact, God will work with them and inspire them deep in their hearts to do so.

This kind of love must begin before a man even meets his future bride. Being responsible means a man commits to his future bride not by use of condoms but by the practice of celibacy. Lust can't wait to take. Love can wait to give. Love can wait until marriage.

A Father Provides

A father provides—I can sum this up in one Scripture verse: "If anyone does not provide for his relatives, and especially for members of his household, he has denied the faith and is worse than an unbeliever" (1 Tim. 5:8). There are no excuses. There is no place to run and hide from that Scripture.

A Father Prepares His Children

A father loves his children when he prepares them for life by teaching them through word and deed. There is a Crosby, Stills, Nash, and Young song whose title says it all: "Teach Your Children."

It became my senior class song. I hope my generation has lived up to it.

This song title echoes the words of Scripture, which encourage parents to teach their children God's ways. "Teach them to your children, talking of them when you are sitting in your house, and when you are walking by the way, and when you lie down, and when you rise" (Deut. 11:19). These words prompted me to seek ways to teach my children about life and about God in the most natural of settings, in the everyday of life. I would always take one of them with me whenever I ran errands. In those most mundane of moments, I'd find ways to show them about life and the ways of the Lord we shared. I taught them while playing on the beach, or walking through a hardware store, or just driving in the car.

A father knows each of his children in their own unique personality and gifts and, yes, their limitations, and he encourages them and points them in the way that their nature wants to grow. He may help push a door open for them here or there, but it is up to them to choose to walk through that door.

Have you noticed how often I quote my father and mother in this book? Will your children value and apply what you show and teach them? Here is a promise that you can lean on: "Train up a child in the way he should go; even when he is old he will not depart from it" (Prov. 22:6).

The greatest way to teach and to lead, of course, is by example. The father is like a navigational waypoint or a lighthouse to his children, especially as they grow older and venture out and have to make bigger and bigger decisions. The father, by his example, sets a standard and sets the course. Your job is to be that lighthouse that never moves.

As the children venture out into the world, they have this look-back sense about them. Is this the moral decision Dad would make? Am I being prudent in this decision, the way he would be? Am I being diligent in my pursuits, the way that he would be?

As they move further and further away from the true north of the compass setting of your life, do they feel that stretch, that tug, that something just does not seem right? Are you that fire on a hill that brings them back?

They look up, and they see. "Hmm, my dad has not wavered in what he stands for or in his example to me. Look how far I have drifted from what he taught me. Am I on the right course?" The further they stray from your instruction and example, the more you are like a rubber band tugging on them, pulling them back to the right path. Sometimes that rubber band breaks, and they are set adrift without a compass. Yet even then, they can still see their father in the distance as that immovable lighthouse, that bright fire on the hill that does not move and is always there for them to show them the way to return.

You may know the story of the ship on a stormy sea that radios to a distant light that it sees. The ensign announces, "This is Her Majesty's frigate approaching on your starboard. Yield to us and make way."

The response comes back: "Request denied."

This time, the ship's captain gets on the radio. "This is Her Majesty's frigate. We repeat our request that you yield."

Again the response comes back: "That is a negative. Request denied."

Finally, the captain comes back again. "This is Her Majesty's frigate! Yield to us so that we may pass. Identify yourself!"

There is a delay in the response, and then he hears the voice crackling: "This is the Eddystone Lighthouse. Request denied."

This is what we need to be as fathers: reliable and unmovable in our example and in what we stand for.

A father like that is listened to because he has earned the right. Whatever sacrifice he asks for, he has already paid ten times over. When he disciplines his children, they respect him because he has earned that moment of discipline by investing countless hours of love and care.

A good father does not let the anarchy of the urgent rule him. He does not let the demanding outside world rob him of the important moments with his family. If a man neglects the important things within his family, those neglected areas will become extremely urgent in time. Put your family first. A good father has learned to take the cares and worries of this world and leave them with the Lord, especially as he returns from his work.

He does not just drop his son or daughter off at baseball practice. He becomes an assistant coach or at least stays to watch some of the practices. And he never misses a game.

A Father Is a Priest

A father is the spiritual leader in the family, and he leads by example. If one of his children wakes up early, that child will always see Dad in his chair, studying the Bible and praying. A father prays over his children and with his children each night at bedtime. He blesses their home with holy water and leads them in prayer at every meal.

He takes them to church on Sunday and makes sure that they excel at altar serving and in CCD. He leads them in the Rosary and guides them through the Church's liturgical calendar. He tells them stories from the Bible and teaches them about the lives of the saints.

He is the guardian over what they see on the TV, on the computer, and on the smartphone.

A man does not just teach his children discipline and expect it; he demonstrates his own discipline.

He demonstrates respect and tenderness to their mother, and he protects her. Dr. Ray Guarendi made this point on my radio show. He said that a man needs to protect his wife from overdemanding children when they get too pushy, loud, or invasive with her. He knows that a woman is not intended to do the work of raising children alone. Teach your children to respect their mother, your wife.

Men, we have a battle for the souls of our children today. This world of confused morality and social-justice warriors and a growing hatred for men will not get better until men lead by example in sacrificial love. Society lays out a quagmire of sinking quicksand. "Everyone who hears these words of mine and does not do them will be like a foolish man who built his house on the *sand*" (Matt. 7:26).

Fathers should be especially attentive to their daughters, affirming them as people, letting them know how beautiful they are.

Fathers let their children know that they are protected, that they can talk to Daddy about anything. There is nothing that they can do or say that will cause him to forsake them.

For a moment, let us focus on the special role that a father plays as his sons come of age, to that transition to being a man. You see, a boy's self-esteem comes from his mommy. But confidence comes from competence imbued by his father in manly skills and deeds.

When boys are little, they hang out with their mom, but there comes a time when their father must launch them into manhood. There needs to come a point, perhaps even an informal rite of passage, when a son is recognized as a man by the Dad and the

Uncles. Indeed, there needs to be a formal or informal rite of passage for sons, but this can't be just a formality. The son's greatest rite of passage is his growing in responsibility for himself and others and the affirmation of that by the men around him.

My wife often comments about the company of men in Hawaii—how there is a real sense, especially among the watermen, of their being a brotherhood. We surf, we spearfish, we sail, we paddle, we outrigger canoe. As we saw earlier, the younger men respect the older men by calling them "Uncle." The uncles watch out for the younger boys and men. They teach and guide them and even school them when they need it.

There was a time here in Waikiki when the *keiki*, the children, were not allowed to surf at a spot in front of my house called Queens. They were relegated with their boogie boards to a surfing spot a few hundred yards away called the Wall. Over time, that has changed, but in those days, it was a real rite of passage for a young man to get to surf at Queens surf break with the men.

Children tend to play in the shore break or paddle out and surf when the surf is not too big. But, at some point in a boy's life, a big day of surf comes along. It is the kind of swell that "separates the men from the boys."

I once told my oldest son, Jeremiah, when he was about ten, that someday I would be sitting on my board on a big day and I would look over, and there he would be, sitting next to me. I would not force him to go out with me. I just let him know that there would come a day when he would want to paddle out to the bigger surf. That day did come, and it came sooner than I expected. I had paddled out, assuming he would surf in the shore break. I had my back to the *aina*, the land, and was looking out at the *makai*, the ocean, waiting for the next big set. Then I just sort of felt him. I looked over, and there he was. That day, he rode big waves, and he gained the respect of the uncles as a waterman. He has gone on to ride waves as big as just about anyone has ever ridden, including one particular day when he dropped into an eighty-five-foot wave.

No one can make a boy into a man or proclaim him to be a man. A boy becomes a man in one simple way: by manning up, by accepting responsibilities, and by being accountable for his actions. There is no other way.

My toughest challenge as a father has been to let go and step away so that my shadow does not fall on my four children, especially my three sons. Trees that grow in the shade of a bigger tree will grow crooked and weak. We have to give our sons room to become men, to make their own decisions, to make mistakes, and to learn from those mistakes. We need to realize that they have a Father in Heaven, and we need to step aside so that they can have that direct relationship with God the Father.

Dads are also aware of where they fail, and we must trust in our heavenly Father to step in where we fail and to be the father that our children need and deserve.

One special note here to those heroic stepdads who step up to the plate in young men's lives and love on them as their own. There is a country song by Elvie Shane that tears me apart. It is the song of a stepdad about his stepson as he sings out the title "He Ain't My Blood but He's My Boy."

> He ain't my blood, ain't got my name,
> But if he did, I'd feel the same.
> I wasn't there for his first steps,
> But I ain't missed a ball game yet.
> And that ain't ever gonna change.
> I could never walk away.

Yeah, he's my son, and that's my choice.
He ain't my blood, but he's my, he's my boy.

We need men to walk in the confidence that God has called them to and empowers them with by His Holy Spirit. Lead your families with servant leadership and God will strongly support you, and at least in your realm, the world will see redemption.

That was how I would remember my father.
There was never a place that he walked that
was not the better for his having passed.
If he cut down one tree he planted two.

—Louis L'Amour, *Jubal Sackett*

Conclusion

God created you as a man. The devil hates that. He wants you to feel that you, as a man, are small, cornered, marginalized, that you just don't measure up. But Jesus does not say that. Jesus shows you that you, as a man, are of incomparable worth because He Himself became a man.

There was no confusion in God's mind when He made you a man. He gave you unique attributes and desires so that you could fulfill and find fulfillment in pursuing the unique call that He has just for you.

Do you want to fulfill your telos? Do you sense that visceral desire deep in your heart, that fire in your belly, placed there by the Holy Spirit to inspire you to experience the exhilaration of being bold and strong, wild and free, and to be the powerful, determined man of virtue that this world so badly needs?

It's a Long Ride Home. Why not make that journey riding tall in the saddle as a man of grit and manly virtue?

Let that horse run.

About the Author

Bear Woznick is a World Champion surfer and certified ninja black belt. He is the host of *The Bear Woznick Adventure* radio program and EWTN's motorcycle-based immersive reality-show series, *Long Ride Home with Bear Woznick*. A Benedictine oblate, Bear is the author of several books, including *A Surfer's Guide to the Soul* and *Deep Adventure: The Way of Heroic Virtue*, published by Sophia Institute Press. He is a sought-after speaker. Learn more about "Bear's Man Cave" and "Bear's School of Manliness" at DeepAdventure.com.

Sophia Institute

Sophia Institute is a nonprofit institution that seeks to nurture the spiritual, moral, and cultural life of souls and to spread the gospel of Christ in conformity with the authentic teachings of the Roman Catholic Church.

Sophia Institute Press fulfills this mission by offering translations, reprints, and new publications that afford readers a rich source of the enduring wisdom of mankind.

Sophia Institute also operates the popular online resource CatholicExchange.com. *Catholic Exchange* provides world news from a Catholic perspective as well as daily devotionals and articles that will help readers to grow in holiness and live a life consistent with the teachings of the Church.

In 2013, Sophia Institute launched Sophia Institute for Teachers to renew and rebuild Catholic culture through service to Catholic education. With the goal of nurturing the spiritual, moral, and cultural life of souls, and an abiding respect for the role and work of teachers, we strive to provide materials and programs that are at once enlightening to the mind and ennobling to the heart; faithful and complete, as well as useful and practical.

Sophia Institute gratefully recognizes the Solidarity Association for preserving and encouraging the growth of our apostolate over the course of many years. Without their generous and timely support, this book would not be in your hands.

www.SophiaInstitute.com
www.CatholicExchange.com
www.SophiaInstituteforTeachers.org

Sophia Institute Press is a registered trademark of Sophia Institute. Sophia Institute is a tax-exempt institution as defined by the Internal Revenue Code, Section 501(c)(3). Tax ID 22-2548708.